## the THIRD edition

# New Headway

## Upper-Intermediate
## **Workbook** with key

Liz and John Soars
Sylvia Wheeldon

**OXFORD**

UNIVERSITY PRESS

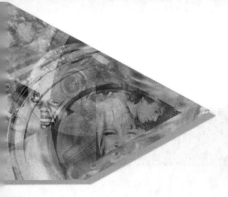

# CONTENTS

You will need to listen to the cassette/CD for some exercises. You can download CD track lists at www.oup.com/elt/headway/tracklists. If you don't have the cassette/CD, you can read the tapescripts on pp83–85.

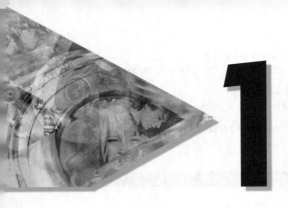

# 1

The tense system
Auxiliary verbs
*have/have got*

**No place like home**

## The tense system

▶▶ **Grammar Reference 1.2 Student's Book p141**

### 1 Identifying tenses

**1** Write in the correct verb form, active or passive, using the verb in the box.

walk

1 **A** How did you get here?

 **B** We walked_____ . It didn't take long.

2 Our baby Jack _____ now. He's a year old.

3 I need to have a rest. We _____ non-stop for four hours.

take

4 It was a hard match. At half-time, one of the footballers _____ to hospital.

5 This shirt fits me. I _____ it.

6 My dog looked guilty. He _____ some food from the kitchen table.

have

7 We need a new car. We _____ this one for ages.

8 We _____ a lovely picnic until my wife was stung by a bee.

9 Don't phone at 8.00. We _____ dinner then.

make

10 Our sandwiches _____ freshly _____ daily.

11 Have you heard about Lenny? He _____ redundant.

12 By the time I'm forty I _____ enough money to retire.

wash

13 **A** Where are my jeans?

 **B** They _____ at the moment.

14 My favourite white T-shirt went pink. It _____ with my daughter's red jumper.

15 Simon was all wet because he _____ the car.

sell

16 My sister earns a good salary. She _____ computer software.

17 If no one offers to buy the house, it _____ by auction next month.

18 I wish I'd bought that antique chair I saw in the shop window. I'm sure it will have been sold by now.

teach

19 At the end of this term I _____ for six years.

20 The children _____ how to make cakes when one boy dropped his bowl on the teacher's foot.

**2** Complete the tense chart with the verb forms from exercise 1.

| Active | Simple | Continuous |
|---|---|---|
| Present | | |
| Past | walked | |
| Future | | |
| Present Perfect | | |
| Past Perfect | | |
| Future Perfect | | |
| **Passive** | **Simple** | **Continuous** |
| Present | | |
| Past | | |
| Future | | |
| Present Perfect | | |
| Past Perfect | | |
| Future Perfect | will have been sold | |

## 2 Correcting mistakes

Correct the sentences.

*I'm working*

1 [X] ~~I work~~ hard at the moment because I have exams next week.

2 [ ] It's really cold lately, so I've bought a new winter coat.

3 [ ] Arsenal play really well at the moment. Their new player has real talent.

4 [ ] I've heard you'll have a baby! Congratulations.

5 [ ] I was doing my homework when my friend was calling.

6 [ ] When I was a little girl, I've always spent my pocket money on sweets.

7 [ ] I went out with Paulo for two years now, and we're still crazy about each other.

8 [ ] I can't decide what to buy my brother for his birthday. Perhaps I'm going to get him a new shirt.

9 [ ] A one-day strike has called by London Underground workers for Friday this week.

10 [ ] The teacher said that Megan had been working hard and was deserved to pass all her exams.

## 3 Choosing the right tense

**T 1.1** Read the telephone conversation between Sophie in New Zealand and Rob in Britain. Put the verbs into the correct tense. Sometimes there is more than one answer.

# Phoning home

**R** Hello?

**S** Rob! It's me! How (1) _____ you _____ (do)?

**R** Sophie? What a nice surprise! Where (2) _____ you _____ (phone) from?

**S** I (3) _____ (stay) in a hotel in Auckland at the moment, and I (4) _____ just _____ (find) this payphone, and I (5) _____ (want) to actually speak to you for a while, so …

**R** Well, it (6) _____ (be) great to hear your voice. I (7) _____ (miss) you so much. I'm glad you (8) _____ (be) home in a few days. I can't wait!

**S** Me, neither. But I (9) _____ (send) you lots of emails and letters, haven't I? I (10) _____ (write) you another long email today, but it isn't finished yet. And I (11) _____ (buy) you some fantastic presents!

**R** Good. I'm glad to hear it! And next time I hope you (12) _____ (not leave) me here and I hope we (13) _____ (be able) to go on holiday together!

**S** Of course we will! But Rob, I (14) _____ never _____ (visit) such a beautiful place in all my life. Do you know where we (15) _____ (go) yesterday? It was a place called Hot Water Beach. It (16) _____ (be) fantastic. We (17) _____ (dig) holes in the sand and (18) _____ (sit) in hot, bubbling water up to our necks!

**R** Sounds amazing! Lucky you!

**S** Oh, I (19) _____ really _____ (look forward) to seeing you again on Friday. See you at the airport at 8.30. Don't forget!

**R** I (20) _____ (wait) there with open arms! Safe journey, sweetie. Love you.

**S** Love you too. Bye.

Hot Water Beach, North Island

## Passives

▶▶ **Grammar Reference 1.2 Student's Book p141**

### 4 Active or passive?

**1** These sentences sound unnatural in the active. Rewrite them using the passive.

1 They built our house in the 17th century.

_____

2 Someone's decorating my flat at the moment.

_____

3 Has someone fixed the coffee machine yet?

_____

4 We ate in restaurants while they were building the new kitchen.
While the new kitchen _____

_____ .

5 We arrived at work to find out that someone had burgled our office.

_____

6 They won't recognize her in those dark glasses.

She _____ .

**2** Put the verbs in brackets into the correct tense, active or passive.

1 The burglars _____ (catch) as they _____ (leave) the office.

2 The postbox _____ always _____ (empty) at 12 midday.

3 Aunt Mary is terribly upset. Her cat _____ (miss) for three days now.

4 We _____ (drive) down a quiet country lane when suddenly we _____ (overtake) by a police car.

5 When I woke up this morning, the world looked magical. It _____ (snow) all night.

6 When you _____ (arrive) in New York, you _____ (pick up) by one of our drivers and taken to the conference centre.

# Living it up!

### 5 Living it up!

**1** Put the verb in brackets into the correct verb form, active or passive, positive or negative. Sometimes there is more than one answer.

A German architect, Werner Aisslinger, thinks that he (1) _____ (find) the answer to our crowded cities. He (2) _____ (invent) a portable micro-apartment. These apartments (3) _____ (call) 'Loftcubes', and they can (4) _____ (lift) onto any empty, flat roof by helicopter!

Each Loftcube (5) _____ (design) with a kitchen and bathroom, as well as a large living area. They are extremely modern – they (6) _____ (build) using all the latest ideas, fabrics, and technology in interior design.

The Loftcube (7) _____ first _____ (show) at an exhibition in Berlin last year, but Berlin (8) _____ (be) the right place for them, because it (9) _____ (have) a housing shortage. These apartments (10) _____ (need) in busy, overcrowded cities, such as London and New York.

They (11) _____ (cost) very much – only £38,000. In the future, Aisslinger hopes that young professionals who often move from city to city (12) _____ (buy) them. When it (13) _____ (be) time to move, they (14) _____ just _____ (take) their home with them!

'Since the Berlin exhibition last year, we (15) _____ (speak) to a number of companies interested in building them, but no decisions (16) _____ (make) yet,' says Aisslinger.

He thinks that the homes (17) _____ (be) ready by the end of next year. Aisslinger's vision of the future is of many rooftop communities in each big city, and it is possible that this way of life (18) _____ (reach) Britain first.

## Auxiliary verbs

▶▶ **Grammar Reference 1.1 Student's Book p140**

### 6 *have, be,* or *do*?

Complete the sentences with the correct form of *have, be,* or *do.* Write **A** for an auxiliary verb and **F** for a full verb. Sometimes the auxiliary is negative.

1 [A] They __*had*__ finished supper when we arrived.
2 [F] We __*had*__ pizza for supper last night.
3 ☐ It _____ been a lovely day. Thank you.
4 ☐ I _____ my homework very quickly yesterday evening.
5 ☐ I always _____ a shower after work.
6 ☐ I _____ always had a passion for Indian food.
7 ☐ Grania overslept, so she _____ catch her train.
8 ☐ What have you _____ to your hair? You look awful!
9 ☐ What _____ your new boyfriend look like?
10 ☐ This self-portrait _____ painted by Van Gogh.
11 ☐ My car _____ being repaired at the moment.
12 ☐ I hate _____ the washing-up. I'd like a dishwasher.

## *have* and *have got*

▶▶ **Grammar Reference 1.1 Student's Book p140**

### 7 Forms of *have* and *have got*

Complete the conversations with a form of *have* or *have got.* Sometimes both forms are possible.

1 **A** Rebecca, _____ you _____ a headache?
   **B** No, it's not that. I _____ a baby and I feel sick.
   **A** Congratulations! Do you want a boy or a girl?
   **B** Well, I _____ three boys, so it would be nice _____ a girl!

2 **A** _____ you _____ any pets?
   **B** No, we _____. _____ you?
   **A** Oh yes. I _____ a dog all my life. At the moment I _____ a dog, two cats, and two mice.
   **B** I'd love _____ a dog, but I'm not so sure about mice!

3 **A** Come on! We _____ hurry. We're late!
   **B** But I _____ my passport. I can't find it anywhere!
   **A** You _____ it yesterday. _____ a look in your bag.
   **B** I _____ it! You were right.

4 **A** I'm looking forward to _____ a few days' holiday. I _____ so much work for the past couple of months, I _____ a break for ages.
   **B** You're lucky! I _____ any holiday left!

**2** Here are the answers to some questions about Werner Aisslinger and his Loftcube. Write the questions.

1 What _____?
   A portable micro-apartment called a Loftcube.

2 Why _____ Loftcubes?
   Because they can be lifted onto any roof by helicopter.

3 Where _____?
   At an exhibition in Berlin last year.

4 _____?
   In busy, overcrowded cities.

5 _____?
   £38,000.

6 _____?
   Young professionals who often move from city to city.

7 Who _____?
   A number of companies interested in building Loftcubes.

8 _____?
   By the end of next year.

# Vocabulary

## 8 Compound nouns

Write one word to make three compound nouns.
Check the use of hyphens in your dictionary.

1 [____] test / pressure / donor

10 [____] works / sign / map

2 [____] cover / case / shelf

11 [____] line / port / mail

3 [____] fall / melon / skiing

12 [____] light / break / dream

4 [____] house / grocer / salad

13 [____] shake / writing / bag

5 [____] club / mare / time

14 [____] cube / berg / rink

6 brief / suit / book [____]

15 birthday / credit / business [____]

7 tea / plastic / shopping [____]

16 [____] scape / lady / slide

8 [____] bow / coat / drop

17 [____] shop / centre / car

9 [____] shine / rise / set

18 note / address / visitors' [____]

'Amazing! But when we go on holiday
one suitcase is too heavy for you.'

## 9 house and home idioms

1 Tick (✓) the correct definition for each idiom. Use your dictionary.

1 *They get on like a house on fire.*
   a ☐ They have a very good relationship.
   b ☐ They are always having arguments.

2 *Help yourself to tea or coffee – make yourself at home.*
   a ☐ Make your own drinks.
   b ☐ Please behave in my house as if it were yours.

3 *Lloyd Webber's new musical brought the house down.*
   a ☐ The musical was a success.
   b ☐ The musical wasn't a success.

4 *The news report really brought home to me the horrors of the famine.*
   a ☐ The report made me realize fully the horrors of the famine.
   b ☐ The report clearly showed the horrors of famine.

5 *His sarcastic comments really hit home.*
   a ☐ He was sarcastic about my house.
   b ☐ His comments really hurt my feelings.

6 *This shaky old bridge is actually (as) safe as houses.*
   a ☐ Don't worry. The bridge is very safe.
   b ☐ Be careful. The bridge isn't safe at all.

2 **T 1.2** Complete the conversations with the idioms from exercise 1 in the correct form.

1 A I was so sorry to hear that your cat had died.
   B Thank you. When I saw her empty bowl, it really _____ the fact that I'd never see her again.

2 A How did the meeting with Andy's parents go?
   B It was great. We all _____ .

3 A Hello! Sorry we're so late, our plane was delayed.
   B Don't worry. Just sit down and relax, and _____ ! I'll put the kettle on.

4 A Did you read those excellent reviews in the local paper about the school play?
   B Yes, I did. Apparently, it _____ !

5 A I'm not going up there. It looks a bit dangerous!
   B Oh, come on! It's _____ , and the view from the top is fantastic!

6 A Why is Terence always so horrible to poor Janine?
   B I don't know. But I could see in her face that his criticisms really _____ .
   Perhaps she'll finally leave him this time.

# Phrasal verbs

## 10 Literal and idiomatic meanings

 Phrasal verbs sometimes have a literal meaning, and sometimes an idiomatic meaning:

*I **looked up** the tree, but I couldn't see my cat.* (literal)

*I **looked up** the spelling in my dictionary.* (idiomatic)

**1** In this exercise the phrasal verbs are all used literally. Complete the sentences with a particle from the box. Some are used more than once.

> away   on   off   back   out   down   in

1 The dentist said my tooth was bad. He had to pull it _____ .

2 Don't run _____ ! Come here! I want to talk to you.

3 My aunt fell _____ the stairs and broke her leg.

4 And I fell _____ my horse!

5 When the sun went _____ it was really cold.

6 A button has come _____ my shirt. Could you sew it back _____ for me?

7 I don't feel like cooking tonight. Shall we eat _____ ?

8 I'm going to the library to take _____ the books I've finished.

9 I've just hung the washing out, and it's starting to rain. Can you help me to bring it _____ ?

10 Don't throw that empty box _____ . I'm sure I can use it for something.

*Jenny and Joe fell out again last night.*

**2** Complete the pairs of sentences with the same phrasal verb from the box in the correct form. Write **L** for a literal meaning and **I** for an idiomatic one.

> take off   fall out   pick up   sort out
> put up   stand up   hold on

1 ☐ After my operation, all my hair _____ . It's growing back now, though.

☐ Jenny and Joe _____ again last night. I could hear them arguing.

2 ☐ I'm coming to London for an interview next week – can you _____ me _____ for the night?

☐ _____ your hand if you know the answer.

3 ☐ I _____ all my clothes drawers today, so now I know where everything is.

☐ We've got a problem here, but if we try hard I'm sure we can _____ it _____ .

4 ☐ When I was at school, we had to _____ when the teacher came in the room.

☐ You shouldn't let your sister tell you what to do all the time. You should _____ for yourself more, and say what you think.

5 ☐ **A** Can I speak to Kate, please?

**B** _____ . I'll just get her.

☐ When you're riding on the back of a motorbike, you have to _____ tight.

6 ☐ It's too warm to be wearing a jumper. Why don't you _____ it _____?

☐ After a slow start, my business finally started to _____ .

7 ☐ I was never taught how to cook. I just _____ it _____ from my mother.

☐ The baby's crying. Can you _____ him _____?

## Pronunciation

### 11 Vowel sounds and sentence stress

1 **T 1.3** Each of these words in phonetics has a different English vowel sound. Write the words. (They are all from Unit 1 of the Student's Book.)

▶▶ **There is a list of phonetic symbols at the back of this Workbook.**

1 /frend/ _____    7 /slæm/ _____

2 /ˈɪŋglɪʃ/ _____    8 /bɒks/ _____

3 /kliːn/ _____    9 /θɔːt/ _____

4 /mʌnθ/ _____    10 /wɜːk/ _____

5 /tʊk/ _____    11 /tʃɑːt/ _____

6 /gruːp/ _____    12 /wɪntə/ _____

2 **T 1.4** This chart shows the main English vowel sounds.

| /e/ | /ɪ/ | /iː/ | /ʌ/ |
|---|---|---|---|
| letter | busy | | |
| | | | |
| | | | |

| /ʊ/ | /uː/ | /æ/ | /ɒ/ |
|---|---|---|---|
| | | | |
| | | | |
| | | | |

| /ɔː/ | /ɜː/ | /ɑː/ | /ə/ |
|---|---|---|---|
| | | | |
| | | | |
| | | | |

Write the words from the box in the correct place on the chart. There are three words for each vowel sound.

| letter | busy | tree | suit |
|---|---|---|---|
| good | cool | sock | camp |
| early | weather | father | floor |
| woman | walk | father | work |
| women | shoe | search | heat |
| machine | mother | daughter | fun |
| machine | building | worry | odd |
| breakfast | want | garden | family |
| could | accent | banana | banana |

## Listening

### 12 A good mate

Jerry

Mike

1 **T 1.5** Listen to the conversation. Mark the sentences true (✓) or false (✗).

1 ☐ Mike and Jerry arranged to meet.
2 ☐ Mike has been away.
3 ☐ Jerry's enjoying work at the moment.
4 ☐ He likes his new boss.
5 ☐ He doesn't want to apply for another job.
6 ☐ He and Sara have enough money for a new car.
7 ☐ Jerry is going to convince Sara that Mike needs a holiday.
8 ☐ Mike is grateful to Jerry.

2 **T 1.5** Listen again and find expressions for these definitions.

1 visit someone unexpectedly _____
2 That's a shame / boring / not fair. _____
3 a very important person _____
4 I don't understand. _____
5 not feel able to do something _____
6 Thanks. _____

3 Look at the tapescript on p83. Find examples of where words have been missed out in informal conversation.

## Present Perfect
### Continuous verb forms
### *have something done*

**Been there, done that!**

# Present Perfect

▶▶ **Grammar Reference: Student's Book p141**

## 1 Present Perfect Simple or Continuous?

**1** Match the lines to make sentences.

| | A | B |
|---|---|---|
| 1 | I've written<br>I've been writing | to Auntie Fay to wish her<br>    happy birthday.<br>my essay all morning. |
| 2 | I've lost<br>I've been losing | weight recently.<br>my car keys. |
| 3 | They've missed<br>They've been missing | you lots, so come home soon.<br>the train. |
| 4 | She's been talking<br>She's talked | on the phone for ages.<br>about this subject before. |
| 5 | Paula's been leaving<br>Paula's left | work early today to meet<br>    her uncle.<br>work late all this week. |
| 6 | The cat's been going<br>The cat's gone | to our neighbour's to have<br>    its dinner.<br>upstairs. |
| 7 | He's had<br>He's been having | a heart attack.<br>second thoughts about<br>    accepting the job. |
| 8 | I've been saving up<br>I've saved up | to buy a new television.<br>about £200. |
| 9 | I've been swimming,<br>I've swum | twenty lengths today.<br>which is why my hair is wet. |
| 10 | I've been finding<br>I've found | my cheque book at last.<br>it difficult to concentrate<br>    recently. |

**2** Put the verbs in brackets into the Present Perfect Simple or Continuous.

1 I **'ve been playing** (play) tennis all morning and I'm really tired.

2 Please drive carefully to work. It _____ (snow) and the roads are very dangerous.

3 How far _____ you _____ (travel) this morning?

4 Kay and Bruno _____ (live) in London for the past five years. Recently they _____ (try) to buy a house in the country, but they _____ (not manage) to sell their flat yet.

5 Jill and Andy _____ (argue) a lot recently, because Jill's always going out with her friends.

6 I _____ (eat) so much ice-cream, I feel sick!

7 The trains _____ (run) late all morning.

8 Cecilia _____ (cry) all day because she _____ (fail) all her exams.

9 I _____ (sunbathe) all morning, and now I've got sunburn.

## 2 Present Perfect and Past Simple

Look at Junko Tabei's personal history. Complete the questions and answers.

### Junko Tabei
#### THE FIRST WOMAN TO CLIMB EVEREST

| Age | |
|---|---|
| 0 — | Born in Fukushima, Japan |
| 4 — | Started at Fukushima Elementary School |
| 10 — | Went mountain-climbing for the first time with her school class |
| 22 — | Joined an all-male mountaineering club |
| 23 — | Graduated from Showa Women's University with a degree in English and American Literature, and devoted herself to mountaineering |
| 26 — | Got married |
| 30 — | Started the first women's climbing club in Japan |
| 32 — | Had her first child, a daughter |
| 36 — | Climbed Mount Everest and received a medal from the King of Nepal |
| 39 — | Had a son |
| 53 — | Became the first woman to climb the Seven Summits (the highest mountain in each of the seven continents) |
| 64 — | Climbed her 113th mountain |

1 Where **was Junko Tabei born?**
   In _____ .

2 Which _____ to?
   **Fukushima Elementary School.**

3 How long _____ climbing?
   Since she _____ .

4 What _____ at university?
   _____ .

5 How long _____ married?
   _____ 38 years.

6 What _____ she was 30?
   _____ .

7 When _____ Mount Everest?
   _____ 36.

8 Who _____ a medal?
   The _____ .

9 How many _____ climbed?
   _____ .

10 Has _____ exciting life?
   _____ .

## Simple or continuous verb forms?

▶▶ **Grammar Reference: Student's Book p141**

### 3 Spider-boy

1 Read about Scott Cory and choose the correct verb form.

# Spider-Boy

JENNIFER CORY (1) *stands / is standing* in Yosemite National Park, California, looking though a powerful telescope. She looks like a bird-watcher, but she (2) *actually watches / is actually watching* her 14-year-old son, Scott, who (3) *climbs / is climbing* the face of a 2,900-foot mountain. He (4) *has climbed / has been climbing* all morning, and he (5) *has nearly reached / has nearly been reaching* the top.

Scott Cory is the American schoolboy rock-climbing sensation. He (6) *has already climbed / has already been climbing* some of the highest, most dangerous rock-faces in the world. He (7) *started climbing / was starting climbing* when he was seven, and he (8) *broke / was breaking* his first record when he was 11. He (9) *became / was becoming* the youngest person to climb the famous 'El Capitan' mountain in one day. He (10) *has been named / has been being named* 'Spider-boy' by the press.

Scott (11) *trains / is training* at least five hours a day, four days a week. He (12) *has prepared / has been preparing* for months for his latest challenge. Next month he (13) *will climb / will be climbing* 'La Esfinge' mountain in Peru. Steve Schneider, 43, his fellow rock-climber, says 'I (14) *haven't seen / haven't been seeing* any other kids do what he does.'

2 **T 2.1** Read Scott's email from Peru. Complete the email with the verbs in the box in the correct form. Decide if the verbs are simple or continuous. Sometimes there is more than one answer.

| do (× 2) | arrive | choose | stay | go | become |
|----------|--------|--------|------|----|--------|
| train | call | be | not be | look | make |
| take | prepare | not enjoy | sound | get | |

Dear Mom and Dad

Lots of love from sunny Peru! I (1) **'m doing** fine so far, and Steve (2) _____ good care of me as usual. We (3) _____ at Lima airport last night. I (4) _____ the flight much. It was very long!

Lima is very hot and crowded, but we (5) _____ only _____ here for one more night. Tomorrow we (6) _____ to 'La Esfinge' to take a look. Steve says that out of all the mountains, here he (7) _____ the hardest climb for us! It (8) _____ 'Welcome to the Slabs of Koricancha'. Funny name, eh?

I think this climb (9) _____ harder than anything I (10) _____ in my life. The high altitude (11) _____ it difficult to breathe. And there (12) _____ many hand and foot holds, because the rock face is so smooth. But I (13) _____ forward to it. It (14) _____ like a lot of fun!

I (15) _____ so hard recently, and I think I (16) _____ enough for this climb. So please don't worry about me. If we (17) _____ to the top, we (18) _____ the first Americans to do it!

Wish me luck, and thanks for everything, Mom and Dad.

Loads of love, Scott

# Passive

▶▶ **Grammar reference 1.2 Student's Book p141**

## 4 Present Perfect passive

1 Rewrite the sentences using the passive and omitting the subject.

1 The postman has already delivered the mail.

The mail _____ .

2 Have the workmen repaired the street lights yet?

_____

3 The government has just passed some new anti-smoking laws.

Some new anti-smoking laws _____

_____ .

4 The local council hasn't built any new homes for twenty years.

No _____ .

5 Nobody has watered the plants.

The plants _____ .

2 Rewrite the newspaper headlines using the Present Perfect passive.

1 **Rat Alert at Buckingham Palace**

Rats have been found in Buckingham Palace.

2 **Dramatic Rescue of Yachtsman in Pacific**

_____

3 **Theft of Valuable Jewels from Sotheby's**

_____

4 **Missing Boy Alive**

_____

5 **Huge Pay Rise for Euro MPs**

_____

6 **Monsoon Kills 260 in India**

_____

7 **Ancient Tomb Discovery in Egypt**

_____

8 **Ferrari Shock – 2,000 Redundancies**

_____

## 5 have something done

 1 Look at the difference in meaning between these three sentences:

*I've repaired* my bicycle. = I repaired it myself.

My bicycle *has been repaired*. = Someone repaired it. It is not important who did it.

*I've had* my bicycle *repaired*. = I arranged/paid for someone to repair it for me. (*have* + object + past participle)

2 *Have something done* is used to talk about services that you ask someone else to do.

I'm going to *have my hair cut*.

1 Rewrite the sentences using *have something done*.

1 John's kitchen is being decorated.

He's having the kitchen decorated.

2 My sister wants someone to pierce her ears.

She wants to _____ .

3 My eyes are going to be tested.

I'm going to _____ .

4 Mr and Mrs Turner's car has been serviced.

They _____ .

5 Our television hasn't been repaired yet.

We haven't _____ .

2 It's Melanie and Ken's wedding day. Look at the notes and write sentences about what they have had / are having done.

She's had her wedding dress made.
He ...
They ...

RECENTLY – wedding dress made
– the invitations printed
– the cake decorated

YESTERDAY – champagne delivered
– hair cut

TODAY – hair done
– flowers delivered

NEXT WEEK – photos developed
– wedding dress dry-cleaned

# Vocabulary 1

## 6 Revision: *make* or *do*?

**1** **T 2.2** Complete the conversations with *make* or *do* in the correct form.

1  **A** How many party invitations do we need?

   **B** Mmm. Let me see. Fifty. That'll (1) _____ fine.

2  **A** Can't you (2) _____ more of an effort with your schoolwork, Joe?

   **B** Well, I'm (3) _____ my best, Dad!

3  **A** What have you bought all that old furniture for?

   **B** I'm going to (4) _____ it up and sell it! I think I'll (5) _____ a nice profit on it.

   **A** Is this what you're going to (6) _____ for a living now? What happened to your job at the bank?

   **B** It was boring. And they asked me to (7) _____ overtime! I'm not working on Saturday mornings, no way.

   **A** But it was a good job! You could've (8) _____ well there.

   **B** Well, I didn't like the manager much. I don't think I (9) _____ a very good impression on him.

   **A** Well, I'm not surprised! You never (10) _____ it to work on time.

   **B** Anyway, you should have seen his face when I told him I was leaving! (11) _____ my day!

   **A** Oh, that (12) _____ it! I can (13) _____ without all your get-rich-quick schemes! I'm going to look for another boyfriend!

'The food's pretty bad here, but we make up for it with exceptionally large portions.'

**2** Complete the sentences with these expressions in the correct form.

| make up for sth | make off with sth |
|---|---|
| make the big time | make sth of sb |
| do without sb | could do with sth |
| make sth in time | |

1  Wow! Look at your name in lights outside the theatre! You've really _____!

2  Thank you so much for helping me! I couldn't _____.

3  **A** What happened to my ham sandwich?

   **B** I'm afraid the dog grabbed it and _____! Sorry.

4  Flowers and chocolates? I know you're trying to _____ forgetting my birthday. But you'll have to try harder than that.

5  I'm really hungry. I_____ a big steak and chips right now.

6  Cathy behaves really strangely sometimes. I don't know what to _____.

7  I'm late! I'll never _____ the station _____!

## Vocabulary 2

### 7 Travel and transport

**1** Tick the verbs which go with each form of transport.

|  | car | bus | bike | train | plane | ship/ferry |
|---|---|---|---|---|---|---|
| get into/out of | | | | | | |
| get on/off | | | | | | |
| take off | | | | | | |
| land | | | | | | |
| ride | | | | | | |
| drive | | | | | | |
| catch | | | | | | |
| miss | | | | | | |
| board | | | | | | |
| park | | | | | | |

**2** Complete the table below with the nouns in the box. Some can go into more than one column.

| | | |
|---|---|---|
| runway | platform | seat belt |
| crash helmet | harbour | carriage |
| traffic lights | life jacket | ticket collector |
| service station | season ticket | trolley |
| tyres | track | horn |
| port | one-way street | check-in desk |
| traffic jam | timetable | hand luggage |
| Customs | deck | tunnel |
| porter | cabin | aisle seat |
| charter flight | cycle lane | cargo |

| car | bus | bike |
|---|---|---|
| | | |
| **train** | **plane** | **ship/ferry** |
| | | |

## Prepositions

### 8 Prepositions of movement

Complete the text with prepositions from the box. Use each preposition at least once.

| | | | |
|---|---|---|---|
| across | against | on | onto |
| along | in | off | into |
| up | out of | over | through |
| past | to | towards | at |

# Joe's journey across town

Joe's plane landed on time (1) _____ Heathrow airport. He had exactly one hour to get (2) _____ the airport and (3) _____ the centre of London to catch his train (4) _____ Manchester. He hurried (5) _____ Customs and passport control and then raced (6) _____ the taxi sign at the exit. Unfortunately, at that moment, the strap on his rucksack broke and it fell (7) _____ his back and (8) _____ the ground. Dirty socks, shirts, and underpants spilt all (9) _____ the airport floor. Joe was so embarrassed! He stuffed everything back (10) _____ his rucksack and, pushing his way (11) _____ the crowds of people, finally made it (12) _____ the taxi rank. He jumped (13) _____ the nearest taxi, shouting 'Euston Station, quickly, please!' The taxi set off at such speed that Joe was thrown forward, hitting his face (14) _____ the glass partition. The taxi sped on and finally arrived (15) _____ the city centre, and inevitably, the middle of a traffic jam! It would be quicker to walk. Joe paid the driver, leapt (16) _____ the taxi and ran (17) _____ the pavement, (18) _____ all the brightly-lit shop windows. At last he could see the station opposite, but it was difficult to get (19) _____ the road because of all the traffic. He reached the station just as his train was leaving. He jumped (20) _____ the barrier, raced (21) _____ the platform and leapt (22) _____ the train with seconds to spare. He sighed with relief – he would be home in time for Christmas.

# Pronunciation

## 9 Word stress

**1** **T 2.3** Here are pairs of words in phonetic script from Student's Book Unit 2. Look at the stress marks. Transcribe them and practise saying them.

1 /ɪkˈsplɔːrə/      /ˌekspləˈreɪʃən/

_____    _____

2 /dʒəˈpæn/      /dʒæpəˈniːz/

_____    _____

3 /kənˈtrɪbjuːt/      /kɒntrɪˈbjuːʃn/

_____    _____

4 /ˈɪndəstri/      /ɪnˈdʌstriəl/

_____    _____

5 /ɪˈkɒnəmi/      /iːkəˈnɒmɪks/

_____    _____

6 /ˈpɒlətɪks/      /pɒləˈtɪʃn/

_____    _____

**2** What is the stress pattern of the words in exercise 1? Write the words in the correct column below.

| ● ● | ● ● ● | ● ● ● |
|---|---|---|
|  | explorer |  |
| ● ● ● | ● ● ● ● | ● ● ● ● |
|  | exploration |  |

**3** **T 2.4** Say these words from Unit 2. Write them in the correct column above.

| | | |
|---|---|---|
| discovery | develop | backpacker |
| information | calculate | abroad |
| destruction | kilometre | unique |
| destroy | unspoilt | Vietnam |
| pollution | industry | environment |
| paradise | European | destination |
| diarrhoea | inhabitant | illegal |

# Listening

## 10 A camping nightmare

**1** **T 2.5** Listen to Sebastian talking to Alex and Marie about his camping trip. Mark the sentences true (✔) or false (✗).

1 ☐ Sebastian is in a good mood.
2 ☐ He took his girlfriend, Tiffany, camping.
3 ☐ She's been camping before.
4 ☐ He was relatively calm in the storm.
5 ☐ She eventually saw the funny side of things.
6 ☐ Sebastian's looking forward to seeing her again.
7 ☐ Marie was very sympathetic to Sebastian during the story.
8 ☐ Alex was very sympathetic about Tiffany during the story.

**2** Who makes these exclamations? Put **A** for Alex, **M** for Marie, and **S** for Sebastian.

1 ☐ Hey, Sebastian! What a surprise!
2 ☐ Whoops!
3 ☐ I mean, how silly!
4 ☐ What a shame!
5 ☐ How awful!
6 ☐ What a nightmare!
7 ☐ Yuck!
8 ☐ What a ridiculous thing to happen!
9 ☐ Phew! What a relief!
10 ☐ What rubbish!

**3** **T 2.5** Listen again. Complete the lines with the fillers you hear.

1 … she turned up with _____ two suitcases and a hairdryer _____ .
2 … she _____ started crying a bit, saying that she was scared. And I was trying to _____ reassure her …
3 … it all went dark, and she _____ freaked out and started running across the field …
4 Well, I ran after her and fell into some _____ disgusting muddy stuff …
5 … and then I started to laugh, _____ really laugh …
6 She caught a taxi and went off … still with the sleeping bag round her and grass and leaves in her hair _____ .

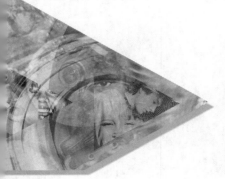

# 3 Narrative tenses
Time expressions

**What a story!**

# Narrative tenses

▶▶ **Grammar Reference: Student's Book p142**

## 1 Irregular verbs

**1** Complete the sentences with the irregular verb in the box in either the Past Simple or the Past Perfect.

fall ☐

1 Harry _____ in love with a Greek girl while he was working in Athens.

2 He _____ in love before, but this was different. He wanted to marry her.

tear ☐

3 Johann saw Camilla's trousers and asked how she _____ them.

4 While she was hiking in the Alps, she _____ her trousers on a rock.

cost ☐

5 It _____ an awful lot to have our car fixed.

6 Ted told me his new car _____ a fortune.

fly ☐

7 When I went to Australia, I was nervous because I _____ (never) before.

8 The plane took off and _____ into the clouds.

catch ☐

9 Suzy wondered how she _____ a cold in the middle of her summer holiday.

10 She _____ a taxi outside the restaurant, and went back to her hotel.

be ☐

11 Talks _____ held in New York last week to discuss global warming.

12 When the politicians left the talks, no decisions _____ reached.

**2** Tick the verbs in exercise 1 which have the same form for the Past Simple and the past participle.

## 2 Past Simple or Past Continuous?

Choose the correct tense.

1 I *lived* / *was living* in Eastbourne when I *met* / *was meeting* my husband.

2 Our team *played* / *was playing* really well. We *won* / *were winning* at half time, but in the end we *lost* / *were losing* 3–2.

3 I *didn't think* / *wasn't thinking* of having a birthday party, but now I'm glad I *had* / *was having* one.

4 I'm so tired. The baby next door *was coughing* / *coughed* all night long and we *weren't getting* / *didn't get* any sleep.

5 Roger *sunbathed* / *was sunbathing* by the hotel pool when he *heard* / *was hearing* a strange sound. An enormous insect *appeared* / *was appearing* and *landed* / *was landing* on his leg.

6 It *was snowing* / *snowed* when I *got up* / *was getting up* this morning. The children next door *made* / *were making* a snowman, so I quickly *put* / *was putting* on some warm clothes and *raced* / *was racing* outside to help them.

7 Jack *was playing* / *played* happily in the snow when his big brother *hit* / *was hitting* him on the head and *made* / *was making* him cry.

*'The kids just played quietly all night, like kids do.'*

## 3 Which narrative tense?

**T 3.1** Complete the article with the verbs in the box.

| Past Simple | | Past Continuous | Past Perfect Simple | Past Perfect Continuous | Present Perfect |
|---|---|---|---|---|---|
| heard | reached | was standing | had been knocked | had been swimming | has been |
| shouted | said | was trying | had taken | had been surfing | have been |
| called | wasn't | were getting | had just finished | | |
| went back in | managed | was recovering | had hit | | |
| had to | felt | | had moved | | |
| was | swam | | | | |
| pulled | | | | | |

# The blind sea hero

## Sightless swimmer saves a surfer

Alec Munroe (1) _had been swimming_ in the sea off the coast near his house in St Ives, Cornwall, and (2) _____ on the beach when he thought he (3) _____ cries for help.

Despite being totally blind, Mr Munroe (4) _____ the sea to rescue the person in difficulties.

'I (5) _____ just in the right place at the right time to help somebody,' the 51-year-old (6) _____ yesterday.

Mr Munroe, who (7) _____ blind for 22 years, (8) _____ to reach Matthew Slade by using the drowning man's cries to guide him. Mr Slade (9) _____ but (10) _____ off his surfboard by a huge wave and (11) _____ his head on a rock. Mr Munroe (12) _____ through rough sea to find him, then (13) _____ Mr Slade and his surfboard back to shore.

Mr Munroe explained, 'I (14) _____ drying myself, when someone (15) _____ 'Help'. I (16) _____ back to him to keep on shouting. I (17) _____ think about the direction of the wind, too. While I (18) _____ to find him, the wind and the waves (19) _____ stronger and stronger. But I just kept going until I finally (20) _____ him and got him back to the shore. It (21) _____ a long time to fight through the high waves, and we (22) _____ completely exhausted.' Last night Mr Slade (23) _____ in hospital from shock and a broken arm.

What was even more remarkable was that Mr Munroe (24) _____ familiar with the coastline. He and his wife (25) _____ to St Ives only two weeks before.

'Fortunately, I (26) _____ a good swimmer all my life,' he said.

## 4 Time expressions

**1** Match the lines and time expressions. Use each expression once only.

| | | | | |
|---|---|---|---|---|
| 1 | **e** I've been working in the same bank | a | ☐ | 10 years ago. |
| 2 | ☐ I started this job | b | ☐ | before my first poem was published. |
| 3 | ☐ I didn't want to get married | c | ☐ | by the time I was 40. |
| 4 | ☐ I had had two children | d | ☐ | until I was 30. |
| 5 | ☐ I'd been writing poetry for many years | e | ☐ | for years. |
| 6 | ☐ I didn't stay in that job | f | ☐ | since six o'clock. |
| 7 | ☐ I've been waiting here | g | ☐ | until I arrived. |
| 8 | ☐ They didn't start ordering the meal | h | ☐ | when he finally arrived. |
| 9 | ☐ The train pulled out of the station | i | ☐ | for long. |
| 10 | ☐ I'd been waiting over an hour | j | ☐ | a minute ago. |
| 11 | ☐ I haven't been feeling well | k | ☐ | until it was too late. |
| 12 | ☐ They got on the plane | l | ☐ | until late. |
| 13 | ☐ I'd never seen him | m | ☐ | lately. |
| 14 | ☐ I was watching TV | n | ☐ | at the last minute. |
| 15 | ☐ He didn't hear the attacker | o | ☐ | before. |

**2** Complete the sentences, using past tenses only and the prompts in brackets.

1 Two years ago, while I _____ .
(work / Paris / grandfather / die)

2 As soon as I _____ .
(feed / cat / do / homework)

3 First I _____ .
(shower / then / dressed)

4 Since I was a child I _____ .
(always / want / visit / Australia / finally / go / last year)

5 As he _____ .
(post / letter / realize / not put / stamp)

6 By the time he'd _____ .
(finish / speak / most / audience / fall asleep)

7 Once I'd _____ .
(tell him / truth / feel better)

8 Until I _____ .
(find a flat / I / stay with friends / months)

# Past passives

## 5 Active to passive

In these sentences the subject is either not important or too obvious to be necessary. Put each sentence into the passive.

1 Someone stole my bike last night.
**My bike was stolen last night.**

2 Archaeologists discovered a Roman temple underneath the new housing estate.

A Roman temple _____

_____

_____ .

3 The sports officials held the races indoors because it was raining.

The races _____

_____ .

4 Someone had booked the leisure centre for a children's party on Saturday.

The leisure centre _____

_____

_____ .

5 The plumber was repairing the dishwasher so I couldn't leave the house.

The dishwasher _____

_____ .

6 When we returned to our hotel room, the chambermaid still hadn't cleaned it.

Our hotel room _____

_____

_____ .

7 The chef hadn't cooked the fish for long enough.

The fish _____

_____ .

8 Workmen were putting up new traffic lights at the crossroads.

New traffic lights _____

_____ .

# Revision of active and passive

## 6 Film review

**T 3.2** Read the review and complete it with a verb in the correct tense, active or passive.

# Fairytale ending

**Shrek 2 is a bit more of the same, but not quite,** says Gerard Cross

| regard | show | feel | like | make |
|---|---|---|---|---|

Don't get me wrong. I liked *Shrek 2*. When the film (1) _____ in cinemas last week, kids and their mums and dads (2) _____ it, too. But the first *Shrek* will be the one that (3) _____ as a classic.

The most striking thing about the original *Shrek* was its freshness. It (4) _____ new and exciting, because of the progress that (5) _____ by the film industry in animation techniques. With *Shrek 2*, of course, there isn't the same surprise.

| marry | tell | rescue | introduce | not make |
|---|---|---|---|---|

The film begins in traditional fairytale style in the Kingdom of Far Far Away, as Prince Charming (voiced by Rupert Everett) (6) _____ the story of how he tried to rescue Princess Fiona from the Dragon. But, of course, Fiona (7) _____ already _____ by our loveable monster Shrek, and what's more, she's (8) _____ him! Now Shrek (9) _____ by his new wife to his parents-in-law. Predictably, he (10) _____ a good impression on the King and Queen (voiced by John Cleese and Julie Andrews).

| base | not write | voice | love | be | end |
|---|---|---|---|---|---|

There are many new characters, by far the best one being Puss-in-Boots, who (11) _____ by Antonio Banderas.

Amusingly, this character (12) _____ on the actor's film role of *Zorro*.

However, the plot (13) _____ by the original creative team, and it shows. The story (14) _____ with a typically Hollywood feel-good message: that whether you (15) _____ black, white, purple, or a green monster, you (16) _____ still _____ for who you are inside. And unfortunately, that's the biggest fairytale of all.

# Vocabulary

## 7 The world of literature

The following words are related to prose, poetry, or drama. Put them into the correct columns. Some words can go in more than one column.

nursery rhyme
plot
chapter
critic
director
backstage
best-seller
script
review
character
leading role
novelist
blockbuster
verse
fairytale
setting
whodunnit
rehearsal
science fiction
hardback
performance
thriller
playwright
autobiography
act
full house
paperback

| Poetry | Prose | Drama |
|--------|-------|-------|
|        |       |       |

# Phrasal verbs

## 8 Type 1 phrasal verbs

 There are four types of phrasal verb. Types 2 and 3 are on p36 in Unit 5 and type 4 is on p48 in Unit 7. Type 1 phrasal verbs consist of a verb + adverb. There is no object.
They can be both literal and metaphorical.
*She stood up and walked out.* (literal)
*The bomb went off.* (metaphorical)

1 Match the phrasal verbs and definitions.

| | | | |
|----|-------------|---|---------------------------|
| 1  | find out    |   | have a calmer, more stable life |
| 2  | break up    |   | wait a minute             |
| 3  | hold on     |   | be quiet                  |
| 4  | speak up    |   | discover                  |
| 5  | set off     |   | be happier                |
| 6  | stay in     |   | not go out, stay at home  |
| 7  | settle down |   | talk louder               |
| 8  | turn up     |   | arrive                    |
| 9  | cheer up    |   | end a relationship        |
| 10 | shut up     |   | begin a journey           |

2 Complete the sentences with the phrasal verbs from exercise 1. Put the verbs in the correct form.

1 Peter hasn't arrived yet – I hope he _____ soon.

2 We have a long journey tomorrow. What time do we have to _____?

3 Why are you so miserable? _____!

4 I don't feel like going out tonight. Shall we _____ and order a pizza?

5 Larry was a bit wild at university, but then he got a job, found a lovely wife, _____ and had kids.

6 After three years of going out together, Josh and Lil eventually _____ because Josh didn't want to get married.

7 Can I copy your homework? The teacher will never _____.

8 _____! I'm trying to watch a programme and you're all talking.

9 **A** What's Bill's phone number?'

  **B** _____! I'll just look it up.

10 _____! We can't hear you at the back!

# Pronunciation

## 9 Diphthongs

> **!** Diphthongs are two vowel sounds which run together.
> **hear** /hɪə/ = /ɪ/ + /ə/ diphthong /ɪə/
> **hair** /heə/ = /e/ + /ə/ diphthong /eə/

▶▶ **There is a list of diphthongs at the back of this Workbook.**

**1** **T 3.3** Choose the correct transcription of each word. What is the other word? Read both aloud.

| | | | | | | | | |
|---|---|---|---|---|---|---|---|---|
| 1 | pay | /peɪ/ | /peə/ | 5 | dear | /dɪə/ | /deə/ |
| 2 | write | /raɪt/ | /rəʊt/ | 6 | boy | /bəʊ/ | /bɔɪ/ |
| 3 | phone | /fəʊn/ | /faɪn/ | 7 | tour | /tʊə/ | /təʊ/ |
| 4 | round | /reɪnd/ | /raʊnd/ | 8 | fair | /fɪə/ | /feə/ |

**2** **T 3.4** Read the poem aloud. Write the number next to the correct sound.

### SOUNDS AND LETTERS DON'T AGREE

When the English tongue we speak,

Why does (1) *break* not rhyme with (2) *weak*?   ☑ /iː/   ☑ /eɪ/

Won't you tell me why it's true

We say (3) *sew*, but also (4) *few*?   ☐ /uː/   ☐ /əʊ/

And the maker of a verse

Cannot rhyme his (5) *horse* with (6) *worse*?   ☐ /ɔː/   ☐ /ɜː/

(7) *Beard* is not the same as (8) *heard*.   ☐ /ɜː/   ☐ /ɪə/

(9) *Cord* is different from (10) *word*,   ☐ /ɜː/   ☐ /ɔː/

(11) *Cow* is cow, but (12) *low* is low,   ☐ /aʊ/   ☐ /əʊ/

(13) *Shoe* is never rhymed with (14) *foe*.   ☐ /uː/   ☐ /əʊ/

Think of (15) *hose* and (16) *dose* and (17) *lose*,   ☐ /uːz/   ☐ /əʊz/   ☐ /əʊs/

And think of (18) *loose* and yet of (19) *choose*,   ☐ /uːz/   ☐ /uːs/

Think of (20) *comb* and (21) *tomb* and (22) *bomb*   ☐ /ɒm/   ☐ /uːm/   ☐ /əʊm/

(23) *Doll* and (24) *roll*   ☐ /ɒl/   ☐ /əʊl/

and (25) *home* and (26) *some*.   ☐ /ʌm/   ☐ /əʊm/

And since (27) *pay* is rhymed with (28) *say*   ☐ /eɪ/   ☐ /eɪ/

Why not (29) *paid* with (30) *said*, I pray?   ☐ /eɪ/   ☐ /e/

Think of (31) *blood* and (32) *food* and (33) *good*;   ☐ /ʊ/   ☐ /uː/   ☐ /ʌ/

(34) *Mould* is not pronounced like (35) *could*.   ☐ /ʊd/   ☐ /əʊld/

Why is it (36) *done*, but (37) *gone* and (38) *lone*?   ☐ /əʊ/   ☐ /ʌ/   ☐ /ɒ/

Is there any reason known?

To sum up, it seems to me

That sounds and letters don't agree.

# Listening

## 10 What an amazing coincidence!

**1** **T 3.5** Listen and answer the questions.

1. What was the programme that Becky saw?
2. What happened to the young mother and her baby?
3. Where was the father?
4. Who got married?
5. What did the father tell his daughter?
6. Where did the daughter move to?
7. Who did she go to have dinner with?
8. Who did she meet?
9. How did her mother feel?
10. What were the amazing coincidences in the story?

**2** **T 3.5** Listen again. Put the phrases for giving and responding to news in the order that you hear them.

a ☐ I don't believe it!
b ☐ Apparently …
c ☑ Did you see that programme about …?
d ☐ Really?
e ☐ Tell me.
f ☐ Actually …
g ☐ Then what happened?
h ☐ That's amazing!
i ☐ Don't tell me that …
j ☐ You're kidding!

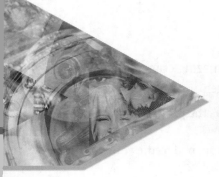

## Questions and negatives
## I don't think you're right

**Nothing but the truth**

# Negatives

▶▶ **Grammar Reference 4.2 Student's Book p144**

## 1 Negative auxiliaries

Complete the sentences with the negative auxiliaries in the box.

| isn't | aren't | 'm not | hasn't | didn't |
|-------|--------|--------|--------|--------|
| doesn't | don't | hadn't | won't | haven't |

1  Jackie speaks fluent French, but I _____ .

2  We wanted to leave the party, but Fred _____ .

3  I've been to America, but my parents _____ .

4  I thought Volvos were made in Austria, but they _____ .

5  They said she was getting better, but she _____ .

6  I'll be moving to London, but my girlfriend _____ .

7  My husband's going to the wedding, but I _____ .

8  Jo likes Indian food, but Andrew _____ .

9  Bill thought I'd forgotten our wedding anniversary, but I _____ .

10  The bedroom's been decorated, but the bathroom _____ .

## 2 no, not, -n't, or none?

Complete the sentences with *no*, *not*, *-n't*, or *none*.

1  I'll help you, but **not** tonight.

2  We have **no** onions left. Sorry.

3  **None** of us understood the lesson.

4  The teacher was**n't** very clear.

5  I asked you _____ to make a mess.

6  Why did _____ you do what I asked?

7  How do you manage _____ to put on any weight?

8  Bring Alessia to the party, but _____ Ben. He's too loud.

9  There's _____ meat in this dish, so it's suitable for vegetarians.

10  **A**  Who likes algebra?
    **B**  _____ me.

11  **A**  Where's the nearest swimming pool?
    **B**  There are _____ around here.

12  She has _____ idea of how to enjoy herself.

13  Why have _____ you emailed me for so long?

14  I can cook, but _____ the way my mother does.

15  **A**  Do you work late?
    **B**  _____ if I can help it.

16  **A**  Where's the coffee?
    **B**  There's _____ left.

17  _____ plants can survive without water.

18  I've got _____ time for people who are rude.

19  _____ of my friends smoke.

20  **A**  Do you like jazz?
    **B**  _____ usually.

## 3 Opposite meanings

Rewrite the sentences to give them the opposite meaning. Make any necessary changes using negative forms and antonyms.

1 She's rich. She's got lots of money.
**She's poor. She hasn't got any money at all.**

2 I told you to go to work. Why are you in bed?
_____
_____

3 Tom was a successful businessman who achieved a lot in his life.
_____
_____

4 Our house is difficult to find. Everybody always gets lost.
_____
_____

5 We had a lovely time in Venice. There weren't many people there.
_____
_____

6 You must exercise your ankle. Try to move it as much as possible.
_____
_____

7 I must iron my shirt. I'm going out tonight.
_____
_____

8 You need to come with me. I won't go on my own.
_____
_____

9 I was in a hurry, because I needed to go to the shops.
_____
_____

10 All of the students passed the exam, so their teacher was pleased.
_____
_____

## 4 I don't think you're right

> 1 In English we usually say *I don't think* + affirmative verb:
>
> >   I **don't think I know** you.
> >   NOT ~~I think I don't~~ know you.
>
> We do the same with *believe*, *suppose*, and *expect*.
>
> >   I **don't expect** we'll **meet** again.
> >   My parents **didn't believe I'd pass** my exams.
>
> 2 We can also use *seem*, *expect*, and *want* with the negative (+ object) + infinitive:
>
> >   She **doesn't** seem **to be** very happy.
> >   I **don't** expect **to get** the job.
> >   I **don't** want to **go back** to that restaurant.
> >   He **doesn't** expect **us to pass** the exams.

Rewrite the sentences, using the verb in brackets in the negative.

1 You haven't met my wife. (I think)
**I don't think you've met my wife.**

2 You haven't got change for a 20-euro note. (I suppose)
_____

3 This machine isn't working. (This machine seems)
_____

4 It wasn't going to rain. (I thought)
_____

5 Their daughter's moving to Canada. They aren't happy. (They want)
_____

6 I'm surprised to see you here. (I expect)
_____

7 You haven't seen Robert recently. (I suppose)
_____

8 I wouldn't like snails. (I think)
_____

9 You probably don't remember me. (I expect)
_____

10 She didn't pass all her exams. (I believe)
_____

# Questions

▶▶ Grammar Reference 4.1 Student's Book p143–144

## 5 Catch me if you can

**T 4.1** Read the text about Frank Abagnale and write questions for the answers.

**Frank Abagnale** was a brilliant conman for five years. Amazingly, he started at 16. Steven Spielberg made the film *Catch Me If You Can* about him, starring Leonardo DiCaprio and Tom Hanks.

In 1964, Frank ran away to New York, upset because his parents had divorced. He was tall and handsome with prematurely greying hair, so he decided to pretend he was 26 to get a job.

His first con trick was to forge bank cheques. When the bank found out, he had already collected $40,000. He had to change his identity, so he became Frank Williams, a Pan Am Airways pilot. He conned Pan Am into giving him a pilot's uniform, and he faked an ID card. For two years he travelled round the world for free with paid hotel expenses! But after he told his secret to his flight attendant girlfriend, she called the police, and he had to disappear again.

Next he became a lawyer. He forged a Harvard law degree, and then studied to pass the bar exam! He was also a hospital doctor (he left when he actually had to treat someone), and a university professor. He taught Sociology and apparently his classes were very popular. Each time he had to move on before the police caught up with him.

He was eventually arrested in France in 1969 and sent to prison for five years.

Since then, he has worked as a financial fraud consultant!

1 <u>How long was Frank Abagnale a con man for?</u>
Five years.

2 _____ ?
Steven Spielberg.

3 _____ to New York?
Sixteen.

4 _____ ?
Because he was upset about his parents' divorce.

5 _____ ?
He was tall and handsome with greying hair.

6 _____ ?
Forging bank cheques.

7 _____ ?
$40,000.

8 _____ ?
Two years.

9 _____ ?
His girlfriend.

10 _____ ?
A lawyer.

11 _____ ?
Sociology.

12 _____ ?
In 1969.

13 _____ ?
Five years.

14 _____ since then?
He's been working as a financial fraud consultant.

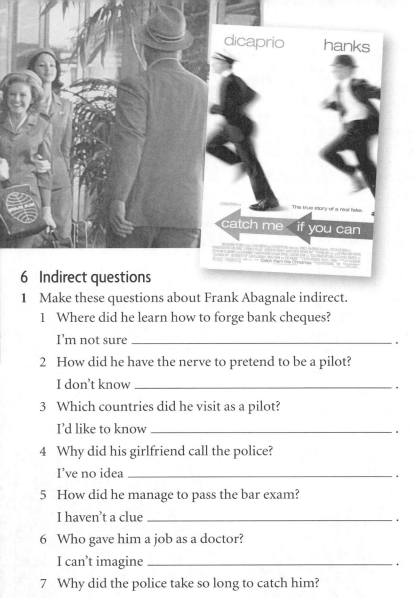

## 6 Indirect questions

**1** Make these questions about Frank Abagnale indirect.

1 Where did he learn how to forge bank cheques?

I'm not sure ——————————— .

2 How did he have the nerve to pretend to be a pilot?

I don't know ——————————— .

3 Which countries did he visit as a pilot?

I'd like to know ——————————— .

4 Why did his girlfriend call the police?

I've no idea ——————————— .

5 How did he manage to pass the bar exam?

I haven't a clue ——————————— .

6 Who gave him a job as a doctor?

I can't imagine ——————————— .

7 Why did the police take so long to catch him?

I wonder ——————————— .

8 What did he think of prison?

Do you know ——————————— ?

**2** Write indirect questions about Frank Abagnale for these answers.

1 I wish I knew ——————————— .

He told her because he loved her and was tired of living a lie.

2 Have you any idea ——————————— ?

It took him three attempts to pass the bar exam.

3 Why do you think ——————————— ?

He went there because he wanted to stop running and settle down in one place.

4 Can you tell me ——————————— ?

He spent five years in prison.

5 Do you know ——————————— ?

He is truly sorry for what he did, and has spent the rest of his life being a model citizen.

## 7 Questions and prepositions

**1** Complete the questions with the prepositions in the box.

| in of by with to from at about ~~for~~ on |

1 What is your home town famous **for** ?

2 Who was that book written ———— ?

3 Who does this dictionary belong ———— ?

4 What are you looking ———— ?

5 What did you spend all your money ———— ?

6 What sort of books are you interested ———— ?

7 What are you talking ———— ?

8 What are you so afraid ———— ?

9 **A** You've got a postcard.

  **B** Oh. Who is it ———— ?

10 Who are you angry ———— ? James or me?

**2** Write a short question with a preposition in reply to these sentences.

1 **A** I went to the cinema last night.
  **B** **Who with?**

2 **A** I'm very cross with you.

  **B** ——————————— ?

3 **A** We're going away for the weekend.

  **B** ——————————— ?

4 **A** I'm very worried.

  **B** ——————————— ?

5 **A** I'm going to Australia.

  **B** ——————— ? Two weeks? A month?

6 **A** I bought a present today.

  **B** ——————————— ?

7 **A** Have you heard? Jane has got engaged.

  **B** ——————————— ?

8 **A** Can you cut this article out for me?

  **B** ——————— ? I haven't got any scissors.

## 8 Negative questions

▶▶ **Grammar Reference 4.2**
**Student's Book p144**

Match a question in **A**
with a line in **B**.

| A | | B | |
|---|---|---|---|
| 1 | Are you ready yet? | a | What have you been doing all this time? |
| 2 | Aren't you ready yet? | b | It's time to go. |
| 3 | Don't you want me to help you? | c | I thought you did. |
| 4 | Do you want me to help you? | d | I will if you want. |
| 5 | Aren't you a member of the tennis club? | e | I'm sure I've seen you there. |
| 6 | Are you a member of the tennis club? | f | If you are, we could have a game. |
| 7 | Don't you know the answer? | g | Yes or no? |
| 8 | Do you know the answer? | h | I'm surprised at you! |
| 9 | Don't you think it's beautiful? | i | Surely you agree with me! |
| 10 | Do you think it's beautiful? | j | I'm asking because I'm not sure. |
| 11 | Didn't I tell you I'm going out tonight? | k | I can't remember now. |
| 12 | Did I tell you I'm going out tonight? | l | I thought I had. Sorry. |

## 9 Can you keep a secret?

**T 4.2** Complete the questions in the conversation.
Use *How come?* once. Sometimes there is more than one answer.

**A** I went to a party last night.

**B** Did you? **Whose**?

**A** Belinda's. You know, my friend from work.

**B** Oh yes. What (1) _____ ?

**A** It was quite good. I chatted to various people.

**B** (2) _____ ?

**A** Well, I talked for a long time to Vicky, you know, from school.

**B** Of course. Brainy Vicky. (3) _____ ?

**A** She's fine. Got a good job. But actually, she's not very happy at the moment.

**B** (4) _____ ?

**A** I don't know if I can tell you. Look, you can keep a secret,
(5) _____ ?

**B** Of course I can. So, what (6) _____ ?

**A** She's having a terrible time with her boyfriend Sam.

**B** (7) _____ ?

**A** You remember. He was a year above us at school.

**B** (8) _____ ?

**A** You know. Quite tall. Dark curly hair. Nice smile.

**B** Oh yes, I remember now. (9) _____ use to wear glasses?

**A** That's right. But he doesn't any more. Anyway, they had been talking about getting married and everything, when suddenly he went all funny and cold towards her.

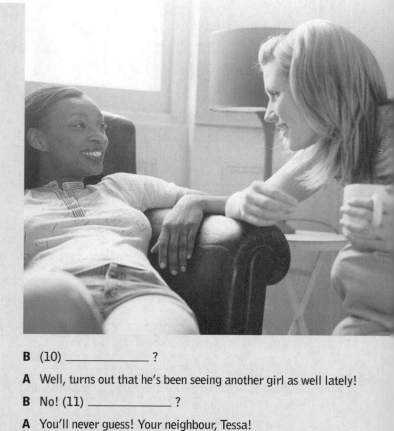

**B** (10) _____ ?

**A** Well, turns out that he's been seeing another girl as well lately!

**B** No! (11) _____ ?

**A** You'll never guess! Your neighbour, Tessa!

**B** Not Tessa! I can't believe it! (12) _____ Vicky _____ now?

**A** She's going to try to forgive him. Apparently, he's very sorry. But don't tell anyone.

# Vocabulary

## 10 Revision: antonyms and synonyms

**1** For the words in **A**, write their opposites in **B**, using prefixes.

| A<br>Adjectives | B | C |
|---|---|---|
| truthful | untruthful | dishonest |
| real | | |
| credible | | |
| plausible | | |
| probable | | |
| pleased | | |
| normal | | |
| professional | | |
| important | | |
| **Nouns** | | |
| honesty | | |
| reality | | |
| belief | | |
| **Verbs** | | |
| appear | | |
| understand | | |
| trust | | |
| cover | | |

**2** In column **C**, write synonyms for the words in **B**, using the words in the box.

| | |
|---|---|
| fake | confuse |
| ~~dishonest~~ | reveal |
| deceit | unbelievable |
| fantasy | vanish |
| ridiculous | annoyed |
| bizarre | amateur |
| unlikely | trivial |
| incredulity | suspect |

## 11 Hot Verbs *keep* and *lose*

**1** Tick the correct column to make expressions with *keep* and *lose*.

| keep | | lose |
|---|---|---|
| ✓ | calm | |
| | weight | ✓ |
| | a promise | |
| | your way | |
| | in touch with sb | |
| | going | |
| | a secret | |
| | sb waiting | |
| | your temper | |
| | fit | |

**2** Complete the sentences with an expression from exercise 1 in the correct form.

1 When you go away, please write. I'd like to _____ _____ with you.

2 When Joe broke the TV, I _____ my _____ and started shouting at him.

3 Can you _____ ? Don't tell anyone, but I'm going to ask Vicky to marry me.

4 Have you been here long? Sorry to _____ you _____ .
I took the wrong road and I _____ my _____ .
I had to ask for directions!

5 **A** I've lost my purse!
**B** Now don't panic. _____ and we'll look for it.

6 I go to the gym every day because I like to _____ .
And I ate so much on holiday that I need to _____ .

'Can you keep a secret?'

HOW TO LOSE WEIGHT

# Prepositions

## 12 Verb + preposition

Many verbs are followed by prepositions. Complete the sentences with the correct preposition.

1 I agree **with** every word you say.

2 I applied _____ the job, but I didn't get it.

3 What are you all laughing _____? What's the joke?

4 He died _____ a heart attack.

5 She's suffering badly _____ sunburn.

6 Do you believe _____ magic?

7 I didn't realize that Maria was married _____ George.

8 Don't you think Mike's been acting _____ a very strange way?

9 Did you succeed _____ convincing your father you were telling the truth?

10 Compared _____ you, I'm not very intelligent at all!

11 We've complained _____ our teacher _____ the amount of homework we get.

12 Stop laughing _____ me. It isn't funny!

13 I've completely fallen _____ love _____ you.

14 Who are you going to vote _____ in the next election?

15 Tom Hanks has appeared _____ 15 major films.

# Pronunciation

## 13 Intonation in question tags

> **T 4.3** In question tags the intonation either falls ↘ or rises ↗.
>
> 1 ↗ Falling intonation means that the sentence is more like a statement = 'I'm sure I'm right. Can you just confirm this for me?'
>
> *It's really warm again today, isn't it?*
> *You've lost the car keys again, haven't you?*
>
> 2 ↗ Rising intonation means that the sentence is more like a real question = 'I'm not sure if I'm right about this. Correct me if I'm wrong.'
>
> *You've been invited to Jane's party, haven't you?*
> *John didn't fail his driving test again, did he?*
>
> Both patterns are very common in spoken English because they invite other people to join in the conversation.

1 **T 4.4** Write the question tags for the statements. Mark whether it falls or rises. ↗

1 You're angry with me, **aren't you** ?

2 Last night was such a hot night, _____ ?

3 You couldn't help me carry this bag, _____ ?

4 Antonio's late again, _____ ?

5 It's cold for this time of year, _____ ?

6 I'm just hopeless at telling jokes, _____ ?

7 You haven't seen my pen anywhere, _____ ?

8 By the end of the film we were all in tears, _____ ?

9 You wouldn't have change for a £10 note, _____ ?

2 **T 4.5** Write a sentence and a question tag for these situations and choose the intonation pattern.

1 You ask Tom if he could help you do your homework.

Tom, **you couldn't help me with my homework, could you** ? ↗

2 You're coming out of a restaurant where you have just had a really tasteless meal with a friend.

That _____ ?

3 You can't believe that your sister has borrowed your new coat again.

You _____ ?

4 You need a neighbour to water your plants while you're away.

You _____ ?

5 You think that Vanessa is going on a business trip to Rome next week, but you're not sure.

Vanessa, you _____ ?

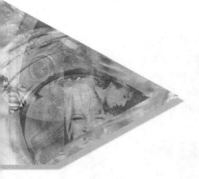

# 5

Future forms
Conjunctions in time clauses

**An eye to the future**

# Future forms

▶▶ **Grammar Reference: Student's Book p144**

## 1 Question tags

Match a sentence in **A** with a question tag in **B**.

| A | B |
|---|---|
| 1 You're going to work harder from now on, | will we? |
| 2 I'll see you next week, | doesn't it? |
| 3 Kate's leaving soon, | won't we? |
| 4 You'll ring when you get there, | are you? |
| 5 Our plane takes off at 4 p.m., | won't I? |
| 6 The decorators will have finished by next week, | isn't she? |
| 7 You aren't getting married next week, | won't you |
| 8 We won't need tickets to get in, | won't they? |
| 9 We'll be millionaires one day, | will he? |
| 10 Max won't be coming, | aren't you? |

I THINK I'LL WAIT FOR IT TO COOL DOWN A BIT!

## 2 *will* or *going to*?

Complete the conversations with *will* or *going to* in the correct form. Sometimes there is more than one answer.

1 **A** I _____ make myself a sandwich. Do you want one?

  **B** No thanks. I _____ have something later.

2 **A** Marco and Lia _____ Florida this year for their holidays.

  **B** How wonderful! The boys _____ love it, especially Disneyland.

3 **A** Bye, Mum. I _____ meet Tom and Mel. I _____ be back at about ten o'clock.

  **B** OK, but don't be late again or I _____ be really annoyed.

4 **A** Jo _____ be furious when she finds out I've crashed the car.

  **B** She _____ understand if you explain that it wasn't your fault.

5 **A** I _____ not _____ work today, I feel awful.

  **B** Don't worry, I _____ ring your boss and tell her you're sick.

6 **A** I'm tired. I think I _____ go to bed.

  **B** I _____ watch the news, then I _____ join you.

7 **A** My boss has told me I _____ be promoted.

  **B** Congratulations! We _____ have to celebrate!

8 **A** Mr Smith, now you've won the lottery you _____ be the fifth-richest man in England. How do you feel about that?

  **B** I _____ tell you next week. I'm too shocked at the moment!

## 3  What does John say?

Write what John actually says in these situations.
Use a future form.

1  He sees some very black clouds in the sky.

John: '**It's going to rain.**'

2  His sister has just reminded him that it is his grandmother's birthday soon.

John: 'I _____ .'

3  He has decided to study hard for his final exams.

John: 'I _____ .'

4  He's made an appointment to see the dentist next Friday.

John: 'I _____ .'

5  He predicts a win for his team, Manchester United, on Saturday.

John: 'I think _____ .'

6  He's stuck in a traffic jam. He's late for a meeting. He rings his office.

John: 'I'm sorry. _____ .'

7  His sister is pregnant. The baby is due next March.

John: 'My sister _____ ,'

8  His plane ticket for next Sunday says:

Departure 7.30 a.m. London, Heathrow.

John: 'My plane _____ .'

9  He can see himself lying on a beach in Spain next week at this time.

John: 'This time next week _____ ?'

10  He predicts hot weather there.

John: 'I think it _____ .'

## 4  Future Continuous or Future Perfect?

Tracey is a student at the moment. Look at her plans for things she thinks she will have done or she will be doing by the time she's forty. Write what she thinks using either the Future Continuous or Future Perfect.

1   move to the States
2   work hard in journalism
3   live in New York
4   pay off my student bank loan
5   earn at least $100,000 a year
6   eat out at least four times a week
7   run in Central Park every day
8   get very fit
9   marry an American
10   have two children

By the time I'm forty …

1  **I'll have moved to the States.**

2  **I'll be working hard in journalism.**

3  _____

4  _____

5  _____

6  _____

7  _____

8  _____

9  _____

10  _____

## 5 Pop star and soap star in the snow

**T 5.1** Choose the appropriate future form. Sometimes both are possible.

....Celeb Update ..... **New York photoshoot** ...................

# Pop star and soap star in the snow

*Celeb Update* meets up with **Kym Manning** and **Jack Deane** in New York at Christmas on the first anniversary of their marriage.

**CELEB UPDATE**  Hello, Kym and Jack. What are you planning to do while you are in New York?

**Kym**  We (1) *'re going to celebrate / celebrate* the fact that we're back together again. And of course we (2) *'ll have bought / 'll be buying* lots of presents for our family!

**CELEB UPDATE**  Yes, you both split up briefly two months ago. What are your plans for the coming year?

**Kym**  The split was my fault. I was spending too much time in the studio and Jack was left looking after my children. I (3) *'ll never leave / 'll never be leaving* my family again for such a long time.

**Jack**  Yes, it was only a temporary split. It (4) *won't happen / isn't happening* again. We love each other and we (5) *'ll be married / 'll have been married* till the end of our days.

**CELEB UPDATE**  Kym, what (6) *will you be doing / will you have done* now that you've left the pop group *HearSing*?

**Kym**  Well, I (7) *'m going to record / 'll record* my own album as I've now got a solo record deal.

**CELEB UPDATE**  Jack, you left our best-loved soap *East Londoners* at the height of your popularity. What kind of parts (8) *will you be looking for / will you have looked for* now?

**Jack**  I (9) *'ll change / 'm going to change* direction. I (10) *'ll do / 'm going to do* serious drama. I (11) *'ve been getting / 'll have got* some interesting offers and I think I (12) *'ll be making up / 'll have made up* my mind which to take by the end of our holiday.

**CELEB UPDATE**  Kym, of course you already have two children from an earlier relationship. Are you planning any more children with Jack?

**Kym**  Jack is already a great father to my two children, and we (13) *'ll have / 'll have had* a child together as soon as the time is right. But for the time being, we (14) *'ll be concentrating / 'll have concentrated* on our new careers.

**Jack**  And I know that in my new career, I (15) *'ll have been able to / 'll be able to* count on the support of my lovely wife.

**CELEB UPDATE**  Thank you. We wish you both luck for the future.

**Jack and Kym**  Thank you. ■

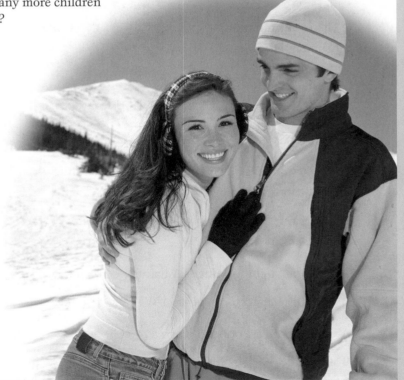

## 6 Correcting mistakes

In these conversations some of the future forms are wrong. Find the mistakes and correct them.

1  ☑ **A** Have you heard? Sue's going to have a baby.

   **I'll**
   ☒ **B** Really? ~~I'm going to~~ give her a ring this evening to congratulate her.

2  ☐ **A** What do you do this weekend?

   ☐ **B** I don't know yet. Maybe I'll give Paul a ring and see what he's doing.

3  ☐ **A** I'll be honest with you, Matthew. I don't think you're going to pass this exam.

   ☐ **B** Oh, no! What will I be doing?

4  ☐ **A** Is it true that Rachel will get married to that awful boyfriend of hers this weekend?

   ☐ **B** I'm afraid so. And I'm going to the wedding. I've got to. I'm her bridesmaid!

5  ☐ **A** Our plane leaves at six o'clock on Saturday morning.

   ☐ **B** Yuk! You have to wake me up. I can never get up in the mornings.

6  ☐ **A** It's my birthday on Sunday. I'm going to be thirty!

   ☐ **B** Thirty! That's ancient! You are getting your pension soon.

7  ☐ **A** Mickey and David will be arriving soon, and the house looks like a pigsty.

   ☐ **B** Don't worry. It'll only be taking a few minutes to clear up.

8  ☐ **A** Will you be going skiing as usual after Christmas?

   ☐ **B** Not this year. It's too expensive. We'll stay at home.

9  ☐ **A** I'll ring you as soon as I'll arrive.

   ☐ **B** Please do. We'll be waiting to hear you've arrived safely.

# Conjunctions in time clauses

## 7 Future time clauses

> ❗ 1 Notice that in clauses after *if*, *when*, *as soon as*, *until*, *before*, *after*, *once*, and *unless* present tenses are normally used to talk about the future. A future form is not used.
>
> *I'll phone you **when I arrive**.* NOT when ~~I'll~~ arrive
>
> *I won't marry you **unless you give up** smoking!*
> NOT unless ~~you'll~~ give up
>
> 2 If it is important to show that the first action will be completed before the second action begins, the Present Perfect is used.
>
> *I'll fax you the report **as soon as I've written** it.*
>
> *They're going to emigrate to Australia **after the baby has been born**.*

Complete the sentences with the verbs in brackets in the correct tense, Present Simple, Present Perfect, or a future form.

1  Unless you _____ (eat) sensibly, you _____ (not get) better.

2  We _____ ( not move) to Paris until we _____ (find) a flat there to rent.

3  You _____ (love) Adam when you _____ (meet) him. He's so funny.

4  _____ you _____ (learn) to drive as soon as you _____ (be) 17?

5  The children _____ ( not go) to bed unless they _____ (have) a glass of milk.

6  It _____ (be) at least an hour before I _____ (finish) this report.

7  If you _____ (not do) well in the test, _____ you _____ (have to) do it again?

8  As soon as we _____ (be) able to process the information, we _____ (deal) with your request.

9  The doctor says that I _____ (feel) much better once I _____ (have) the operation.

10  Once you _____ (try) 'Glowhite' toothpaste, you _____ (never use) anything else!

# Vocabulary

## 8 Revision: *take* or *put*?

**T 5.2** Complete the conversation with the correct form of *take* or *put*.

**A** Come in. Make yourself at home. (1) _____ some music on. Pour us some drinks.

**B** Thanks, I will. Mmm, something smells nice.

**A** Oh, dinner's (2) _____ ages. Go and sit down. (3) _____ your feet up and (4) _____ it easy. It'll be a while before we eat. How's your week been?

**B** Hellish. My boss is (5) _____ pressure on me to (6) _____ on another project. But I'm already working flat out and I'm fed up with (7) _____ work first all the time.

**A** I don't blame you. But the business has really (8) _____ off recently, hasn't it?

**B** Yes, it has, which is great, of course. But I think he'll just have to realize that he needs to (9) _____ on more people now. But he'll never (10) _____ advice from me, of course!

**A** Well, you've been there since the beginning and I think he just (11) _____ you for granted.

**B** I know. I'm like part of the furniture. I have trouble getting him to (12) _____ any notice of me at all these days.

**A** Oh, don't (13) _____ it personally. I'm sure he doesn't mean it like that. He's just too busy, that's all.

**B** Perhaps you're right. But he should (14) _____ himself in my shoes once in a while, and realize how he makes me feel.

**A** You'll just have to talk to him about it. Anyway, this'll (15) _____ a smile on your face. Dinner is served!

## 9 Words commonly confused

Complete the sentences with the correct word. Put the verbs into the correct forms.

**expect    wait for    look forward to**

1  a  We _____ the rain to stop so that we can play tennis.
   b  The weather forecast says a lot of rain _____ over the next few days.
   c  I'm very excited. I'm _____ starting my first job.

**pass    spend    waste**

2  a  I _____ too much time with my mates and not enough time with my girlfriend.
   b  I usually read the newspaper to _____ the time on train journeys.
   c  I _____ my time at school. I wish I'd tried harder and studied more.

**see    watch    look at**

3  a  _____ you _____ that new Spielberg film yet?
   b  The police sat in their car. They _____ every move the men made.
   c  _____ this picture little Amy has painted!

**actually    at the moment    really**

4  a  **A** What a shame James lost the match.
      **B** _____ , he won.
   b  The children are out playing in the garden _____ .
   c  Love that dress. You _____ look wonderful!

**lend    borrow    owe**

5  a  I have a student loan. I _____ the bank £10,000, which is a big debt.
   b  Jed _____ £5,000 from the bank to buy a new car.
   c  Could you _____ me £20 until the end of the week? I'm broke.

**angry    nervous    embarrassed**

6  a  He felt _____ when he realized that he couldn't remember her name.
   b  I'm very _____ about my interview tomorrow.
   c  We're _____ with the government for not listening to us.

# Phrasal verbs

## 10 Types 2 and 3

> ❗ **1** Both type 2 and type 3 phrasal verbs have an object.
>
> | Type 2 | Type 3 |
> |--------|--------|
> | *Take off **your coat**.* | *Look after **your sister**.* |
> | *I put **the DVD** on.* | *I'll look into **the problem**.* |
>
> **2** In type 2, the particle can move.
>
> > *Take your coat **off**.*
> > *I put **on** the DVD.*
>
> If the object is a pronoun (him, it, me, etc.) the particle comes after it.
>
> > *Take it **off**.* NOT ~~Take off it.~~
> > *I put it **on**.* NOT ~~I put on it.~~
>
> **3** In type 3, the particle cannot move.
>
> > NOT ~~Look your sister after.~~
> > ~~Look her after.~~
> > ~~I'll look the problem into.~~
> > ~~I'll look it into.~~
>
> **4** Dictionaries usually tell you which type a phrasal verb is.
>
> **put sth on** The particle is shown *after* **sth**. This is type 2.
> **look into sth** The particle is shown *before* **sth**. This is type 3.

Put a pronoun in the correct place in these sentences. First decide which type of phrasal verb is used.

1 Listen to this song. I'll put **it** on _____ for you.

2 I know you've got a lot of problems, but I'm sure you'll get _____ through **them** .

3 I can't remember the directions. I couldn't take _____ all in _____ .

4 There's a problem with my computer. I'll sort _____ out _____ tomorrow.

5 We're having a meeting on the 25th. Put _____ in _____ your diary.

6 There are clothes all over your bedroom. Please put _____ away _____ .

7 If you're going out with your little brother, you'd better look _____ after _____ .

8 I'm sorry you had a complaint about your room. I'll look _____ into _____ right away.

9 That was a mean thing you said! Take _____ back _____ !

10 I liked Ann, but since you told me what she did, you've put me _____ off _____ .

# Pronunciation

## 11 Sounds and spelling

**1** 〖 T 5.3 〗 Match the letters underlined in each word with the correct sound.

| | | | | |
|---|---|---|---|---|
| 1 | w**o**n't | /ʌ/ | /əʊ/ | /ɒ/ |
| 2 | w**a**lk | /ɔː/ | /ɑː/ | /ɒ/ |
| 3 | w**o**nder | /ʌ/ | /ɔː/ | /ɒ/ |
| 4 | w**o**man | /ʊ/ | /əʊ/ | /ʌ/ |
| 5 | w**a**rm | /ɔː/ | /aɪ/ | /ɜː/ |
| 6 | w**o**rd | /ɔː/ | /ɜː/ | /aɪ/ |
| 7 | w**ea**r | /eə/ | /e/ | /iː/ |
| 8 | w**ei**ght | /aɪ/ | /eɪ/ | /e/ |
| 9 | w**a**nt | /æ/ | /əʊ/ | /ɒ/ |
| 10 | w**o**rk | /ɔː/ | /ɜː/ | /ɔɪ/ |
| 11 | w**a**nder | /ʌ/ | /ɔː/ | /ɒ/ |
| 12 | w**o**men | /ʊ/ | /əʊ/ | /ɪ/ |
| 13 | w**o**rm | /ɔː/ | /ɔɪ/ | /ɜː/ |
| 14 | w**a**rd | /ɑː/ | /aɪ/ | /ɔː/ |
| 15 | w**ea**ry | /eə/ | /ɪə/ | /iː/ |
| 16 | w**ei**rd | /aɪ/ | /eɪ/ | /ɪə/ |

**2** 〖 T 5.4 〗 In each group of words, three words rhyme. Choose the odd one out.

| | | | | | |
|---|---|---|---|---|---|
| 1 | /ʌ/ | done | phone | won | son |
| 2 | /ʊ/ | would | should | good | blood |
| 3 | /uː/ | move | love | prove | groove |
| 4 | /əʊ/ | though | through | throw | sew |
| 5 | /eɪ/ | weak | break | ache | shake |
| 6 | /aʊ/ | flower | power | tower | lower |
| 7 | /ɜː/ | worth | birth | north | earth |
| 8 | /eɪ/ | hate | wait | weight | height |
| 9 | /ɪə/ | fear | near | pear | clear |
| 10 | /eə/ | share | bear | fair | hear |

*'I'm going to pick somebody up at the airport. Anybody.'*

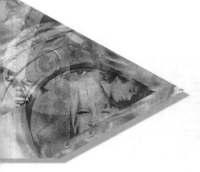

# 6

Countable and uncountable nouns
Expressing quantity
*something, somebody, somewhere*

**Making it big**

## Countable and uncountable nouns

▶▶ **Grammar Reference: Student's Book p146**

### 1 Countable or uncountable?

Choose the noun in each group that is usually uncountable.

1  holiday   journey   flight   luggage   suitcase
2  meal   dish   food   menu   dessert
3  cheque   coin   cash   salary   bonus
4  job   employee   boss   unemployment   profession
5  pop group   musical   music   opera   concert
6  arrest   violence   accident   crime   criminal
7  motorway   traffic   traffic jam   hold-up   rush hour

Choose the noun in each group that is usually countable.

8   luck   happiness   opportunity   fun   help
9   ingredient   cutlery   fruit   meat   food
10  fresh air   sleep   fluid   health   energy

### 2 *some* or *any*?

Complete the sentences with *some* or *any*.

1  I did exercise 1 without _____ help.

2  Would you like _____ more fizzy mineral water?
    I don't want _____ more.

3  _____ people don't have _____ problems learning
    foreign languages.

4  Why don't you ask your father to lend you _____
    money? I haven't got _____ .

5  My teenage sister never has _____ difficulty learning
    the words of the latest pop songs. There are hardly
    _____ she doesn't know by heart.

6  I didn't realize that there was still _____ food left.
    I've made _____ more.

### 3 *much* or *many*?

Rewrite the sentences using the words in brackets and
*much* or *many*. Make any other necessary changes.

1  I'm not sure how much drink to buy. (cans of beer)
   **I'm not sure how many cans of beer to buy.**

2  Are there many jobs to be done in the garden? (work)
   _____

3  I didn't spend many hours on the homework. (time)
   _____

4  Did they do many experiments before they found a
   cure? (research)
   _____

5  They couldn't give me many details about the delay in
   our flight. (information)
   _____

6  I didn't have too much difficulty with this exercise.
   (problems)
   _____

7  I've got too many suitcases. I can't carry them all.
   (luggage)
   _____

8  There are too many cars and lorries on the streets of
   our town. (traffic)
   _____

## 4 The canteen

1 Look at the picture of the students' canteen. Write ten sentences, using each expression in the box once.

| several | a couple of | a few | isn't much |
| lots of | aren't many | a little | hardly any |
| no | a huge amount of | | |

1 _____
2 _____
3 _____
4 _____
5 _____
6 _____
7 _____
8 _____
9 _____
10 _____

2 **T 6.1** Answer the students' questions, using an expression of quantity without a noun.

1 Is there any chocolate cake?
   Sorry, there's **none** left.

2 What about rice?
   Well, there's **a little** .

3 Can I have some spaghetti?
   Yes, of course, there _____ .

4 Have you got lots of ham sandwiches?
   Well, there are _____ .

5 I'd like two vegetable curries, please.
   Sorry, there _____ left.

6 Can I have some chips with my hamburger?
   Sorry, there _____ .

7 Have you got apple pie today?
   Yes, just _____ .

8 Are there any chocolate biscuits?
   Well, there _____ .

9 Can I have a large portion of fruit salad, please?
   Sorry, there _____ left.

10 Are there any bananas left?
   Yes, I think we _____ .

11 Is this all the apple juice you've got?
   Yes, I'm afraid there's only _____ .

12 Well, I'll have some grapefruit juice.
   No problem, we've got _____ .

## 5 very little, a little, very few, a few, fewer, less

Rewrite the sentences with *very little*, *a little*, *very few*, *a few*, *fewer*, or *less*. Change all the underlined words.

1 There was a lot of wine at the party, but <u>hardly any</u> was drunk. **very little**

2 I'm on a diet so I'll just have <u>four or five</u> chips.

3 Children <u>don't</u> have <u>as much</u> respect for their teachers <u>as</u> they used to.

4 Lots of people have tried to climb Everest, but <u>not many</u> have succeeded.

5 Dave can speak fluent Norwegian and <u>some</u> Swedish.

6 <u>Not as many</u> people smoke these days.

7 <u>Not many</u> people manage to become completely fluent in a language.

8 It's been <u>three or four</u> years since we last saw him.

9 There <u>isn't</u> very <u>much</u> I can do to help you.

10 There are lots of reasons why I don't want the job. Here are <u>some</u> of them.

# Compounds with *some, any, no, every*

## 6 *something, anybody, nowhere, everyone …*

> 1 *Any, anyone, anybody, anywhere,* and *anything* can mean it doesn't matter which/who/where/what.
>
> > Put the picture **anywhere**, I don't mind.
> > You can say **anything** you want. I don't care.
> > Borrow **any** book you want.
>
> 2 *Everybody* and *everything* are singular, not plural.
>
> > **Everybody** knows who did it.
> > **Everything** is ready for the party.

**1** Complete the sentences with a combination of these words.

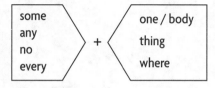

1 I don't care where we go on holiday as long as it's _____ hot.

2 Does _____ want a cup of tea?

3 I've looked for my contact lens, but I can't find it _____ .

4 **A** What do you want for dinner, Harry?

   **B** Oh, _____ , I don't care!

5 This sale is fantastic. There's 50% off _____ in the shop.

6 It's really boring at Auntie Martha's, there's absolutely _____ to do.

7 I'm a very sensitive person. _____ understands me.

8 There was _____ for me to sit so I had to stand.

9 Jane's getting married to _____ she met on holiday.

10 Sue is such a chatterbox, she's always got _____ to say, but she never says _____ interesting.

11 Our dog will go for a walk with _____ .

12 Tommy's so nice. _____ likes him.

**2** Match a line in **A** with a line in **B**.

| A | | B | |
|---|---|---|---|
| 1 | He told the police he knew | a | anything. |
| 2 | He didn't tell the police | b | nothing. |
| 3 | I think they live | c | somewhere in London. |
| 4 | I don't mind. I'll live | d | anywhere in London. |
| 5 | Anybody | e | phoned you. Sorry. |
| 6 | Nobody | f | can cook. It's easy. |
| 7 | I've searched | g | anywhere. |
| 8 | I can't find it | h | everywhere. |
| 9 | I thought I'd know | i | somebody at the party. |
| 10 | I didn't know | j | anyone at the party. |
| 11 | My parents never took me | k | everywhere when I was young. |
| 12 | My parents took me | l | anywhere when I was a kid. |
| 13 | Jane always got | m | everything she wanted. |
| 14 | Jane didn't have | n | anything to wear. |
| 15 | I've already had | o | something to eat. |
| 16 | I've had | p | nothing to eat. |

'Of course nobody needs one, that's why I called you advertising people in.'

## Expressing quantity

### 7 Odonga uses his loaf

1 Read and complete the story of Odonga Bosko, using the words in the boxes.

# Odonga uses his loaf *

---

| a couple   multi   much   few   little   nobody |

Odonga Bosko hasn't had (1) _____ luck in his life – until now, that is. And (2) _____ could have predicted how completely his life would change.

(3) _____ of months ago, 20-year-old Odonga had (4) _____ chance of escaping the grinding poverty in his remote Ugandan village. Now the excited trainee printer is busily packing his (5) _____ belongings for his trip to Britain, because a (6) _____-millionaire is paying for him to study the latest printing techniques at college.

| any   hardly any   more   all   a bit   part   enough |

Remarkably, Odonga's extraordinary change in fortune is (7) _____ because of a loaf of bread. He explained: 'I was hungry, but there wasn't (8) _____ food in the house. I had (9) _____ money – only 600 shillings (4p), but it was just (10) _____ to buy (11) _____ of bread. The bread is usually wrapped in paper, and that day I saw it was (12) _____ of an English paper, so I took (13) _____ notice.

| none   piece   more than   any   something   no |

On the (14) _____ of paper was an advert for a printing job in Bristol. (15) _____ of my friends have (16) _____ work here. I am training on a printing machine which is (17) _____ 40 years old, and I receive (18) _____ wages. I felt if I was going to make (19) _____ of my life, I had to apply for this job.'

| over   a lot   all   several   some   a great deal of |

It took Odonga (20) _____ hours to write the letter and send it. But it turned out that the advert had been placed (21) _____ a year ago. 'The company kindly sent me (22) _____ of information about (23) _____ the hi-tech machines they used. I was even more determined to get a chance to work on them.'

In Britain, Odonga's story reached the ears of Conrad Millbank, a tycoon who had made (24) _____ money from publishing. He ordered his lawyers to find the enthusiastic young African. 'When I heard that a rich man wanted to pay for my training, I thought it must be a joke. Now I am so happy that I went to buy (25) _____ bread that day.'

---

* *to use your loaf* is an idiom meaning *to use your brains / show intelligence.*

## Vocabulary

### 8 A piece of cake!

1 What combinations can you make using nouns from the two columns?

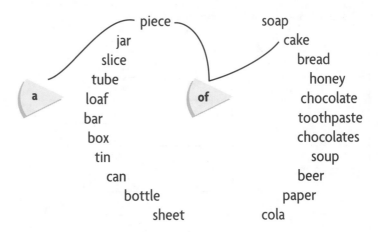

| a | | of | |
|---|---|---|---|
| piece | | | soap |
| jar | | | cake |
| slice | | | bread |
| tube | | | honey |
| loaf | | | chocolate |
| bar | | | toothpaste |
| box | | | chocolates |
| tin | | | soup |
| can | | | beer |
| bottle | | | paper |
| sheet | | | cola |

**2** These sentences contain false information about the article. Correct the mistakes.

1 Odonga has quite a lot of money.

**Odonga has hardly any money.**

2 600 shillings is quite a lot of money.

_____

3 Odonga has few friends.

_____

4 Most young people in his village have jobs.

_____

5 It didn't take him much time to write his letter.

_____

6 There were some jobs available at the company.

_____

7 No-one heard about his story.

_____

8 Until now, Odonga has had quite a lot of good fortune in his life.

_____

**2** Replace the words in italics with combinations from exercise 1.

1 Would you like *some cake*?

_____

2 All we've got for lunch is *some soup*.

_____

3 There are two clean *pieces of paper* on my desk.

_____

4 Don't forget to buy Mum *some chocolates* for Mother's Day.

_____

5 Do you want this *chocolate*? It's plain and I only like milk.

_____

6 There's only one *bit of bread* in the bread bin.

_____

7 How *much beer* have we got left over from the barbecue?

_____

8 Hello, reception? This is room 401. There's not a single *bit of soap* in the bathroom here.

_____

9 We brought you *some* special *honey* back from the country.

_____

# Prepositions

## 9 Prepositions and nouns

**1** Which prepositions go with the words on the right in these two tables?

| A | | | | | |
|---|---|---|---|---|---|
| **above** | **below** | **on** | **over** | **under** | |
| ✓ | ✓ | ✓ | | | average |
| | | | | | foot |
| | | | | | arrest |
| | | | | | £500 |
| | | | | | 75% |
| | | | | | freezing |
| | | | | | 18 years old |
| | | | | | new management |
| | | | | | holiday |
| | | | | | pressure |
| | | | | | business |

| B | | | | | |
|---|---|---|---|---|---|
| **at** | **by** | **during** | **in** | **on** | |
| ✓ | ✓ | | | | midnight |
| | | | | | the night |
| | | | | | New Year's Day |
| | | | | | the winter |
| | | | | | Friday afternoon |
| | | | | | the weekend |
| | | | | | time |
| | | | | | a fortnight's time |
| | | | | | the rush hour |
| | | | | | his forties |

**2** Complete the article with prepositions from exercise 1.

## Who's that girl?

**R**emember **Gisele Bundchen**, the half-German, half-Brazilian model who came to fame (1) _____ the late 1990s, when she was still (2) _____ eighteen years old? (3) _____ the next five years, her face appeared in (4) _____ a hundred magazines and fashion campaigns. (5) _____ five feet ten inches tall, she was slightly (6) _____ average height for a fashion model, but she still had the sassiest strut on the catwalk, earning (7) _____ average $7,000 an hour.

But (8) _____ the height of her career she decided to walk away from all of that, turning down (9) _____ 90 % of her forthcoming projects. (10) _____ her year-long absence, she went (11) _____ winter holidays with her family and Hollywood heart-throb boyfriend, Leonardo DiCaprio, and acted in her first film.

People wondered whether she had been (12) _____ too much pressure or she was working (13) _____ new management, but apparently not. The 23-year-old is making a fashion comeback, but (14) _____ her own time. She wants to be more selective and creative, and is aiming for longevity in the short-lived fashion world. So, still expect to see her (15) _____ her fifties!

# Listening

## 10 A business problem

**1** [T 6.2] Listen to the phone call. Who is calling who? What's the problem?

*John Barker*

**2** [T 6.2] Listen again and mark these sentences true ✓ or false ✗.

1 ☐ John Barker and Ellen Miles know each other.
2 ☐ John Barker's secretary confirmed the order.
3 ☐ Deliveries take more than a week.
4 ☐ The order code is FED 20547/80498 MX.
5 ☐ The order was placed on 1 September.
6 ☐ John Barker is going to call Ellen Miles later that morning.

**3** Who says these things? Write **R** (receptionist), **E** (Ellen Miles), or **J** (John Barker).

1 ☐ Will you hold?
2 ☐ How are things?
3 ☐ Bear with me a moment.
4 ☐ Are you ready?
5 ☐ What was it again?
6 ☐ I'll read that back to you.
7 ☐ Something's come up.
8 ☐ I'll expect your call.

**4** Look at the tapescript on p84 and find equivalent expressions for these phrases:

1 Who do you want to speak to?
2 I'm connecting you.
3 an order I made
4 no more than a week
5 Do you have the order code with you?
6 that all seems to be correct
7 I'll phone you again before 12.

# Pronunciation

## 11 Shifting word stress

**1** [T 6.3] Listen to the pronunciation of the words. Write **N** for noun and **V** for verb.

1 ☐ refuse          7 ☐ permit
2 ☐ transport       8 ☐ record
3 ☐ produce         9 ☐ contract
4 ☐ decrease        10 ☐ desert
5 ☐ progress        11 ☐ present
6 ☐ insult          12 ☐ content

**2** Read this news item aloud. Pay attention to the shifting stress on words that are both verbs and nouns.

'Good evening. Here is the news.

Oil imports continued to increase in the last quarter. Demand for transport fuel is already at record levels, and the Prime Minister refuses to permit any further increases. Members of the Transport Workers' Union objected to his criticisms. They insisted they will protest against any possible future sanctions. They presented a report maintaining that present fuel increases are due to a decrease in investment in railway transport by the government.'

**3** [T 6.4] Listen and check. Practise reading the text again.

**4** Read this news item and mark the stress. Then read it aloud, again paying attention to the shifting stress.

'Exports increased in the last quarter due to the present buoyant economy. Ministers are content with the results, saying that they reflect the progress made in decreased regulation for small businesses.

Tax refunds are on the increase as invalid assessments multiply in the tax office. Tax officers protested against the criticism levelled against them, saying that they were insulted by suggestions that they were not able to produce the correct results. They said they were compiling a report which would present in minute detail the problems they were experiencing since the computer contract had been placed with another company.'

**5** [T 6.5] Listen and check. Practise reading the texts again.

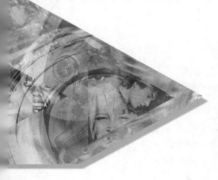

# 7 Modal auxiliary verbs and related verbs
*need*

**Getting on together**

## Revision of all modals

▶▶ **Grammar Reference: Student's Book p147**

### 1 Meaning check

Choose the correct explanation for each of these modals.

1 Amy may look for a new job.
  a [X] Amy has permission to look for a new job.
  b [✓] It's possible Amy will look for a new job.

2 I couldn't swim until I was 16.
  a ☐ I wasn't allowed to swim until I was 16.
  b ☐ I wasn't able to swim until I was 16.

3 No one can smoke in the cinema.
  a ☐ No one is able to smoke in the cinema.
  b ☐ No one is allowed to smoke in the cinema.

4 You should wear glasses.
  a ☐ My advice is that you wear glasses.
  b ☐ It's possible that you will have to wear glasses.

5 Will you answer the phone?
  a ☐ Are you at some time in the future going to answer the phone?
  b ☐ I'm asking you to answer the phone.

6 I couldn't get the top off the jar.
  a ☐ I wasn't allowed to get the top off the jar.
  b ☐ I didn't manage to get the top off the jar.

7 You must be tired.
  a ☐ I'm sure you are tired.
  b ☐ You are required to be tired.

8 Andy's very busy so he may not go to the party.
  a ☐ Andy doesn't have permission to go to the party.
  b ☐ There's a possibility Andy won't go to the party.

### 2 Which modal?

1 Complete the sentences with correct words from the box. Often there is more than one answer.

| will | should | can | ought to | could |
|------|--------|-----|----------|-------|
| must | may | have to | might | |

1 You _____ get your hair cut. It's too long.

2 _____ I ask you a question?

3 Young children _____ be carried on this escalator.

4 You _____ never get a seat on this train. It's always packed.

5 I _____ be studying Mandarin Chinese next year.

6 I _____ already speak five languages fluently.

7 You'll _____ work much harder if you want to pass.

8 It's Saturday night. There _____ be something good on TV.

9 You _____ leave your valuables in the hotel safe.

10 You _____ be over 1m 60 cm tall to be a flight attendant.

2 Choose the correct answer.

1 You *mustn't / won't* have any problems with Jack. He's such a good baby.

2 You *don't have to / mustn't* use cream in this sauce, but it makes it much tastier.

3 I *couldn't / wouldn't* watch my favourite TV programme because Mia rang up for a long chat.

4 Timmy's so stubborn. He just *can't / won't* do what he's told.

5 I'm afraid I *can't / may not* come to your wedding as I'll be in Australia.

6 I *was able to / could* get 20% off the price in the sale.

7 You *don't have to / mustn't* say a word about this to your mother. It's a surprise.

## 3 Positive to negative

Rewrite the sentences to make them negative.

1 You must stop here. _____

2 We must learn the whole poem. _____

3 They had to take off their shoes. _____

4 He must be speaking Swedish. _____

5 We had to wear a uniform at school. _____

6 You'll have to help me do this exercise. _____

# Verbs related to modals

## 4 Online helpline

1 **T 7.1** Read the problem page and replace the words in italics with a modal verb, or an expression with a modal verb.

# *Online helpline*

**Your questions answered confidentially**

 *Email* Noelie Jones

---

From: James, Dudley

**Subject: She's designer-label obsessed**

I'm really worried about my friend. She (1) *always feels it's necessary to have* the latest designer clothes. And she's getting worse. Now, if something isn't from the 'right' label, she (2) *refuses to* allow it in the house. She's losing touch with reality. She (3) *promised to* come round for coffee with me the other day, but then (4) *wasn't able to* because (5) *it was necessary for her* to go to a fashion show. As a good friend, (6) *is it a good idea if* I talk to her about it?

**As a good friend, (7) *it is essential that you* talk to her about it. This label thing is certainly concealing a strong inferiority complex and (8) *maybe she'll* find it hard to discuss it. But if you (9) *manage to* persuade her that she is loveable without designer gear, then you (10) *are certain to* do her a huge service.**

---

From: Charlene, Liverpool

**Subject: I'm desperate to give up smoking**

We (11) *aren't allowed to* smoke at work, which I find difficult. We (12) *'re obliged to* leave the building when we want a smoke, but we (13) *'re only able to* do this twice a day. I go out three or four times, but I know I (14) *'m bound to* get caught sooner or later. I think I (15) *'d better* give up before I lose my job. What do you suggest?

**Choose a day and just stop. (16) *It's possible that you'll* find it difficult at first, but persevere. (17) *It's very necessary that you don't* give in to temptation. When I stopped a few years back, I (18) *wasn't able to* stop thinking about cigarettes, but bit by bit it got better. (19) *If I were you, I'd* try nicotine patches. (20) *It is essential that* you make the most of your current determination. Good luck!**

**2** Rewrite the sentences using the prompts.

1 It's Anna's birthday tomorrow, so I should buy her a card.
   ('d better) _____

2 Guests shouldn't leave valuables in their room.
   (advised not) _____

3 You can only smoke in designated areas.
   (Smoking … permitted) _____

4 I'm sure he'll pass the exam. He's so clever.
   (bound) _____

5 You can't use dictionaries in this exam. (The use of dictionaries … allowed) _____

6 People under 18 shouldn't drink alcohol.
   (supposed) _____

7 Travellers to the States need a visa.
   (required) _____

8 I expect you'll find it difficult to learn Chinese.
   (likely) _____

9 I can't come out. I said I'd help Jane.
   (promised) _____

10 I wasn't allowed to go out until I was eighteen.
   (parents … let) _____

# Modal verbs of probability

## 5 Present probability

**1** Respond to the statements or questions using the words in brackets. Put the verb in its correct form.

1 Harry is packing his suitcase. (must, go on holiday)
   **He must be going on holiday.**

2 Jenny looks really unhappy. (must, miss, boyfriend)
   _____

3 Who's at the front door? (will, Tom)
   _____

4 Where's Kate? It's nearly lunchtime! (can't, still, sleep)
   _____

5 Why are all the lights on in their house? (could, have, party)
   _____

6 James has been working all night. (must, deadline to meet)
   _____

7 It's been snowing all night. (might, difficult, drive, work)
   _____

8 Timmy can't find his little sister. (may, hide, in the garden)
   _____

**2** Complete the conversations with the correct form of the verbs in brackets.

1 **A** You really (1) _____ (should / go) to bed now, or you (2) _____ (might / feel) tired tomorrow.

   **B** I'll go in a minute. I (3) _____ (must / finish) this revision first.

   **A** You (4) _____ (will / pass) the exam easily. Get some rest now.

2 **A** It's five past eleven. Ken and Cathy's plane (5) _____ (should / touch down) in Kennedy Airport right now.

   **B** Your watch (6) _____ (must / be) slow. It's nearly half past.

   **A** It (7) _____ (can not / be)! I've just had it repaired.

3 **A** Bring very warm clothes. It (8) _____ (could / snow) when we arrive.

   **B** Oh, yes. I've heard it (9) _____ (can / snow) in the mountains even in summer.

4 **A** What are all those people doing with those lights and cameras?

   **B** They (10) _____ (must / make) a film.

   **A** Who's the leading man?

   **B** Not sure. It (11) _____ (might / be) him over there. And do you think that she's the leading lady?

   **A** She (12) _____ (could / be). She's certainly beautiful enough!

# need

## 6 need

> **Need** can work like a normal verb or a modal auxiliary verb.
>
> 1  It usually has the forms of an ordinary verb + infinitive with *to*.
>
> > She **needs to go** to bed.
> > Does she **need to go** to bed?
> > She doesn't **need to go** to bed.
>
> 2  It is used as a modal verb mainly in the negative.
>
> > She **needn't go** to bed yet.
>
> But can sometimes be used as a question.
>
> > **Need** I **go** to bed?
>
> 3  *Need + -ing  =  need + passive infinitive*
>
> > *The car needs fixing.  =  The car needs to be fixed.*

**1**  Mark the sentences with **M** when *need* is used as a modal verb, and **V** when *need* is used as an ordinary verb.

1  ☐ I need to go home.
2  ☐ You needn't come if you don't want to.
3  ☐ Ian doesn't need to pass all his exams to get a place at university.
4  ☐ Money is desperately needed to protect the world's endangered species.
5  ☐ Need I pay now, or can I pay later?
6  ☐ If you have any problems, you only need to tell us and we'll try to help.
7  ☐ The garden needs watering.
8  ☐ Leave the washing-up. You needn't do it now.

**2**  Choose the correct verb. Sometimes two are correct.

1  I *mustn't / needn't / don't have to* do this exercise but it might help.

2  You *mustn't / needn't / don't have to* think I'm always this irritable. I've just had a bad day.

3  We *mustn't / needn't / don't have to* book a table. The restaurant won't be busy tonight.

4  Do you really *must / need to / have to* go now? Can't you stay a bit longer?

5  You *mustn't / don't need to / don't have to* eat all your vegetables. Just have the carrots.

6  Have I *must / need to / got to* ring and confirm my room reservation?

7  My bike *needs / must / has to* replacing. Look at the state of it!

# Vocabulary

## 7 Money

**1**  Match the words or expressions in **B** with a word or expression in either **A** or **C**.

| A | B | C |
|---|---|---|
| I opened | My deposit account | will take ages to pay off. |
| I changed | a savings account. | is good just now. |
| He accumulated | His debts | is overdrawn. |
| She contributes | debts of £2,000. | expires at the end of July. |
| I earned £2,000 | Inflation | went up by 2%. |
|  | to the household bills. |  |
|  | in interest. |  |
|  | My credit card |  |
|  | some traveller's cheques. |  |
|  | The exchange rate |  |

**2**  Read the story and choose the most suitable words.

**Ben** stood at the (1) *check-in / check-out* at the supermarket as the assistant (2) *summed / added* up his (3) *bill / fees*. It came to £72.67 and she asked him how he would like to (4) *pay / cost*.

Ben didn't have much money in his deposit account because he hadn't been paid his monthly (5) *wages / salary* yet, so if he paid (6) *by cheque / in cash* he would be (7) *overdrawn / overdue*. Then he realized he had left his (8) *credit card / traveller's cheques* at home. And he couldn't afford to pay (9) *cash / money* because he only had £60.

The shop assistant told him that if he exchanged many of the items he had bought for the shop's own brand he would (10) *reduce / accumulate* his bill by as much as 25%. So Ben set off round the store again.

His new bill (11) *added / came to* only £56.50 – a (12) *saving / discount* of £16.17. Ben got £3.50 (13) *change / coins* from his £60 and his new (14) *receipt / recipe*.

# Phrasal verbs

## 8 Type 4

1. Type 4 phrasal verbs have a verb + adverb + preposition. The preposition has an object.

   Do you **get on with** your neighbours?

   We've **run out of** sugar.

2. The word order cannot change.

   Do you **get on with** them?

   NOT ~~Do you get on them with?~~

   We've **run out of** it.

   NOT ~~We've run out it of.~~

3. Dictionaries show type 4 phrasal verbs by giving both the adverb and the preposition.

   **get away with sth**

4. Sometimes a phrasal verb can be type 4 or type 1. Dictionaries show this.

   **break up (with sb)**

   They **broke up** after five years' marriage.

   She's sad because she's just **broken up with** her boyfriend.

Complete the sentences with the combinations in the box.

| away with | off with (× 2) | up for | up with | out of |
|---|---|---|---|---|
| on with (× 2) | out with (× 2) | ~~up to~~ | down on | |

1. Joey! You've got a very guilty look on your face! What naughty things have you been getting **up to** this time?

2. The burglar broke into the house and made _____ a lot of jewellery.

3. We must try to cut _____ the amount of money we spend a month. We spend more than we earn.

4. Don't let me disturb you. Carry _____ your work.

5. I'm sorry we didn't get into the cinema. I'll take you to a restaurant to make _____ it. Does that cheer you up?

6. There is a move in Britain to do _____ the monarchy completely, so that Britain would become a republic.

7. Sam's mean with money, and he's always trying to get _____ paying his fair share of the bills for the flat.

8. I went _____ Aimee for two years, and then she suddenly went _____ someone else without saying anything!

9. I can't stand Paul. I can't put _____ his rudeness a minute longer. I'm leaving him.

10. Judith's a very difficult person to get _____ . She's always having rows with people and falling _____ them. I'm leaving her.

I can't stand Paul. I'm leaving him.

Judith

BREAKING UP

Judith's a very difficult person. I'm leaving her.

Paul

# Listening

## 9 Not getting on

**1** **T 7.2** Listen to the conversation and choose the best answer.

1 Sophie's upset about ...
- a ☐ her friend.
- b ☐ the evening.
- c ☐ her boyfriend.

2 Charlie's ...
- a ☐ ignored her.
- b ☐ been mean to her.
- c ☐ laughed at her.

3 Charlie's ...
- a ☐ out of work.
- b ☐ having problems at work.
- c ☐ looking for a new job.

4 Anya wants Sophie to ...
- a ☐ leave him.
- b ☐ be nice to him.
- c ☐ tell him to stop it.

5 Sophie ...
- a ☐ agrees to this.
- b ☐ doesn't want to, because she loves him.
- c ☐ wants things to get magically better.

6 After talking to Annie, Sophie feels ...
- a ☐ miserable.
- b ☐ more cheerful.
- c ☐ annoyed.

**2** **T 7.2** Listen again and complete these sentences.

**Understatement**

1 I'm just _____ , that's all.

2 He made _____ remarks this evening.

3 He's been having _____ recently.

4 It's getting me _____ , I must say.

5 Our relationship _____ lately.

**3** Look at the tapescript on p84 and check your answers. Find some examples of exaggeration.

# Pronunciation

## 10 Consonant clusters

English has many words with groups (or clusters) of consonants:

| happened | /hæpnd/ |
| couldn't | /kʊdnt/ |
| puzzles | /pʌzlz/ |

**T 7.3** Say these words from Unit 7 aloud and then transcribe them. They all have consonant clusters.

1 /dʌznt/ _____
2 /ʃʊdnt/ _____
3 /mʌsnt/ _____
4 /prɒmɪst/ _____
5 /stræpt/ _____
6 /dɪstɪŋktli/ _____
7 /speʃl/ _____
8 /əreɪndʒd/ _____
9 /rɪleɪʃnʃɪp/ _____
10 /kʌmftəbl/ _____
11 /ɪksaɪtmənt/ _____
12 /ɪmprest/ _____

## 11 Sentence stress

**T 7.4** Alan and Kevin are chatting about Frank. Read the conversation aloud and mark the stress in Kevin's responses.

1 **Alan** Don't you think Frank's put on a lot of weight recently?

  **Kevin** You're kidding. If anything, he's lost weight.

2 **Alan** I think Frank earns more than me.

  **Kevin** Well, I know he earns a lot more than me.

3 **Alan** He's thinking of buying a second-hand Mercedes.

  **Kevin** What do you mean? He's already bought a brand new one.

4 **Alan** He's just bought two pairs of designer jeans.

  **Kevin** Didn't you know that all Frank's clothes are designer labels?

5 **Alan** Does Frank have many stocks and shares?

  **Kevin** He has loads of them.

6 **Alan** Isn't Frank in New York on business?

  **Kevin** No, in fact he's in Florida on holiday.

7 **Alan** His latest girlfriend has long, blonde hair.

  **Kevin** Really? The girl I saw him with had short, brown hair.

# 8

Relative clauses
Participles

**Going to extremes**

## Defining and non-defining relative clauses

▶▶ **Grammar Reference 8.1 Student's Book p149**

### 1 General knowledge quiz

Test your general knowledge. Tick (✓) the correct answer.

### General Knowledge Quiz on

# extremes

1 **Death Valley,**
   a ☐ *which is in Arizona,*
   b ☐ *which is in California,*
   c ☐ *which is in Texas,*
   **is officially the hottest place on Earth.**

2 **Concorde was …**
   a ☐ *the fastest plane that has ever flown.*
   b ☐ *the longest plane that has ever flown.*
   c ☐ *the only commercial plane that could go faster than sound.*

3 **Belgian Georges Simenon,**
   a ☐ *who was author of the Maigret detective stories,*
   b ☐ *who was author of the Poirot detective stories,*
   c ☐ *who was author of the Philip Marlow detective stories,*
   **wrote over 450 books – the most prolific author last century.**

4 **Kilimanjaro is a mountain in Tanzania**
   a ☐ *which is also the highest summit in Africa and Asia.*
   b ☐ *which is also the highest summit in Africa.*
   c ☐ *which is also the highest summit in the world.*

5 **The tallest building that was built last century was**
   a ☐ *the Sears tower in Chicago.*
   b ☐ *the Petronas Towers in Kuala Lumpur.*
   c ☐ *the Jin Mao building in Shanghai.*

6 **The highest waterfall in the world, which is called**
   a ☐ *the Angel Falls,*
   b ☐ *the Niagara Falls,*
   c ☐ *the Victoria Falls,*
   **is in Venezuela.**

7 **Bambuti pygmies, who only live in the African rainforest,**
   a ☐ *are the tallest people in the world.*
   b ☐ *are the smallest people in the world.*
   c ☐ *are the thinnest people in the world.*

8 **The driest place on Earth is the Atacama Desert,**
   a ☐ *which is in Egypt.*
   b ☐ *which is in Europe.*
   c ☐ *which is in Chile.*

## 2 Defining or non-defining?

1 Decide if these sentences are best completed with a defining relative clause (D), or a non-defining relative clause (ND). Write **D** or **ND** in the boxes.

1 ☐ I'd love to meet someone _____ _____ .

2 ☐ We're looking for a house _____ _____ .

3 ☐ We went to see *Romeo and Juliet* _____ _____ .

4 ☐ Do you know a shop _____ _____ ?

5 ☐ Marilyn Monroe _____ _____ died of a drug overdose.

6 ☐ I find people _____ difficult to get on with.

7 ☐ My computer _____ is already out of date.

8 ☐ I met a girl _____ .

9 ☐ Professor James Williams _____ _____ will give a talk next week.

10 ☐ I bought a ham and pickle sandwich _____ _____ .

2 **T 8.1** Complete the sentences in exercise 1 with this information. Add a relative pronoun and commas where necessary. Leave out the relative pronoun if possible.

> You went to school with her.
>
> I ate it immediately.
>
> It has four bedrooms.
>
> I bought it just last year.
>
> They lose their temper.
>
> It sells second-hand furniture.
>
> Her real name was Norma Jean Baker.
>
> This person could teach me how to cook.
>
> I really enjoyed it.
>
> Many people consider him to be the world's expert on volcanoes.

## 3 Punctuation and omitting the pronoun

Add commas to these sentences if they have a non-defining relative clause. Cross out the pronoun, if possible, in the defining relative clauses.

1 *Sheila, who I first got to know at university, was one of six children.*

2 *The man ~~who~~ you were talking to is a famous artist.*

3 *This is the story that amazed the world.* (no change)

4 The thing that I most regret is not going to university.

5 My two daughters who are 16 and 13 are both interested in dancing.

6 The town where I was born has changed dramatically.

7 I didn't like the clothes which were in the sale.

8 Salt that comes from the sea is considered to be the best for cooking.

9 Salt whose qualities have been known since prehistoric times is used to season and preserve food.

10 The CD that I bought yesterday doesn't work.

11 The part of Europe where I'd most like to live is Portugal.

12 The Algarve where my mother's family comes from is famous for its beautiful beaches and dramatic coastline.

## 4 All relative pronouns

**1** Match a line in **A** with a line in **B**.

| A | B |
|---|---|
| 1 Have I told you recently | when you expect to arrive. |
| 2 I have to do | where my brother lives. |
| 3 We were stuck in traffic for seven hours, | which came as a bit of a surprise. |
| 4 We're emigrating to Australia, | whose hair came down to her waist. |
| 5 I met a girl | how much I love you? |
| 6 I passed all my exams, | whatever you want. |
| 7 Let me know | which was a nightmare. |
| 8 Being generous, I'll buy you | what I believe to be right. |

**2** Complete the sentences with a relative pronoun. If the pronoun can be omitted, add nothing.

1 The lady _____ is sitting in the wheelchair is my grandmother.

2 I know an Italian restaurant _____ serves excellent pasta.

3 I know an Italian restaurant _____ you can always get a table.

4 Uncle Tom earns a fortune, _____ is why I've asked him to lend me £1,000.

5 Sean is a child _____ people immediately like.

6 My daughter, _____ ambition is to emigrate to Australia, has finally got her visa.

7 I gave him a glass of water, _____ he drank thirstily.

8 The flight _____ we wanted to get was fully booked.

9 My auntie's house is the place _____ I feel most at home.

10 This is the smallest car _____ has ever been made.

11 That's the man _____ wife left him because he kept his pet snake in their bedroom.

12 I love the things _____ you say to me.

13 I go shopping at the new shopping centre, _____ there's always free parking.

14 She told me she'd been married before, _____ I didn't realize.

15 _____ you do, don't touch that button. The machine will explode.

## 5 Prepositions in relative clauses

Combine the sentences, keeping the preposition after the verb in the relative clause.

1 I want you to meet the people. I work with them.
**I want you to meet the people I work with.**

2 She's a friend. I can always rely on her.

_____

_____

3 That's the man. The police were looking for him.

_____

_____

4 She recommended a book by Robert Palmer. I'd never heard of him.

_____

_____

5 You paid £400 for a suit. It has been reduced to £200.
The suit _____

_____

6 This is the book. I was telling you about it.

_____

_____

7 The Prime Minister gave a good speech. I agree with his views.

_____

_____

8 He spoke about the environment. I care deeply about this.

_____

_____

9 What's that music? You're listening to it.

_____

_____

10 My mother died last week. I looked after her for many years.

_____

_____

# Participants

▶▶ **Grammar Reference 8.2 Student's Book p150**

## 6 Participles as adjectives

Complete the adjectives with -*ed*
or -*ing*.

1 a shock**ing** story

2 a reserv**ed** seat

3 scream____ children

4 a satisfi____ customer

5 a disgust____ meal

6 a confus____ explanation

7 a house in an expos____ position

8 a conceit____ person

9 a frighten____ film

10 an exhaust____ walk

11 disappoint____ exam results

12 a tir____ journey

13 an unexpect____ surprise

14 disturb____ news

15 a thrill____ story

16 a relax____ holiday

17 a disappoint____ customer

18 well-behav____ children

19 a promis____ start

20 a cake load____ with calories

## 7 Participle clauses

1 Rewrite the sentences with a present or past participle clause instead
of a relative clause.

1 Can you see the woman who's dressed in red over there?

   **Can you see the woman dressed in red over there?**

2 People who live in blocks of flats often complain of loneliness.

   _____

3 Letters that are posted before 5 p.m. should arrive the next day.

   _____

4 The train that is standing on platform 5 is for Manchester.

   _____

5 Firemen have rescued passengers who were trapped in the accident.

   _____

6 They live in a lovely house that overlooks the River Thames.

   _____

7 It took workmen days to clear up the litter that was dropped by the crowds.

   _____

2 Complete the sentences with a verb from the box in either its present or past
participle form.

| feel borrow explain say ~~ruin~~ study finish take know steal |
|---|

1 Jo was in a bad mood for the whole week, completely **ruining** our holiday.

2 After _____ her exams, Maggie went out to celebrate.

3 Jewellery _____ in the robbery has never been recovered.

4 I got a letter from the Tax Office _____ that I owe them £1,000.

5 _____ hungry, I decided to make myself a sandwich.

6 Books _____ from the library must be returned in two weeks.

7 Not _____ what to do, she burst out crying.

8 I had a long talk to Jack, _____ why it was important for him to
work hard.

9 _____ everything into consideration, I've decided to give you a
second chance.

10 With both children _____ at university, the house seems really quiet.

# Revision of relatives and participles

## 8 The thrill seeker

**T 8.2** Read and complete the article with the clauses in the box.

| Relative clause |
| --- |
| a where temperatures drop to –71°C |
| b who battles with |
| c who sees that as a challenge |
| d that nature ever invented |
| e in which there is a lake of boiling lava |
| f where everyone else is |
| g no-one has done before |
| h you've never heard of before |
| i which unexpectedly develops |

| Past participle |
| --- |
| j otherwise known as |
| k Trapped for five days |

| Present participle |
| --- |
| l before heading for the high winds |
| m starting this Monday on the Discovery Channel |
| n getting right inside the 150mph winds |

# The thrill seeker

## He laughs in the face of common sense. He is …
### DANGERMAN

'It helps to be fearless.'

So says Dangerman, (1) ____ extreme adventure cameraman, Geoff Mackley, (2) ____ some of the most inhospitable weather conditions and desolate places (3) ____ . What drives the New Zealander to do it?

'There aren't many places left where no-one has ever been, or things (4) ____ , and I'm one of those people (5) ____ !' he says.

See for yourself in his series of daredevil adventures, (6) ____ .

---

EPISODE 1 **The Perfect Storm**
■ Dangerman chases after major typhoons, first in Asia, (7) ____ of North Carolina, and finally (8) ____ of Hurricane Isabel.

---

EPISODE 2 **The Deep Freeze**
■ In the coldest town on earth in Northern Siberia, (9) ____ , Dangerman and extreme survival expert Mark Whetu become the first people to camp outside!

---

EPISODE 3 **The Crater's Edge**
■ Dangerman climbs down into a volcano, (10) ____ , and gets caught in a tropical storm (11) ____ into a cyclone. (12) ____ with no food or water, he survives torrential rain, violent winds, and clouds of toxic gas.

■ Dangerman says: 'Who wants to be (13) ____ ? It's the thrill of finding a place (14) ____ . More people have landed on the moon than have been to these places.'

# Vocabulary

## 9 People, places, and things

**1** Complete the table with these descriptive adjectives. Put six in each group.

| | | | | |
|---|---|---|---|---|
| ~~unspoilt~~ | stubborn | breathtaking | thrilled | spoilt |
| aggressive | picturesque | automatic | hand-made | deserted |
| exhausted | accurate | waterproof | desolate | long-lasting |
| priceless | easy-going | overcrowded | | |

| People | Places | Things |
|---|---|---|
| | _unspoilt_ | |
| | | |
| | | |
| | | |
| | | |
| | | |

**2** Complete the sentences with an adjective from exercise 1.

1 The view from the top of the mountain was absolutely _____ – fantastic scenery as far as the eye could see.

2 These flowers are quite _____ , if you keep the vase full of water and in the shade.

3 The new car we bought is fully _____ . I don't want to change gears when I'm driving any more.

4 You're good to be on holiday with. You're very _____ , and don't worry about anything.

5 The countryside we camped in was completely _____ – not a person, a gift shop or a caravan site for miles.

6 The Cotswolds is an area in England which is very _____ . It has lots of pretty, old-fashioned villages and beautiful green countryside.

7 Their child is really _____ . He won't do a thing they tell him. I think it's because he's _____ . They give him everything he asks for.

8 That bag you're looking at is _____ . Look at the quality of the work.

9 The beach was seriously _____ . There was no room to put our towels down. So we hired a boat and sailed along the coast until we found a tiny one which was completely _____ . We were the only ones on it!

## 10 Nouns in groups

 Look at these examples of number + noun + noun.

*a three-mile walk*

*a sixteen-year-old girl*

*a ten-hour flight*

These are expressions of measurement before a noun. The number and the first noun are joined with a hyphen, and the first noun is usually in the singular.

Put the information before the noun.

1 a note that is worth ten pounds

_____

2 a language course that lasts four weeks

_____

3 a drive that takes three hours

_____

4 a meal that consists of three courses

_____

5 a holiday that lasts two weeks

_____

6 a delay at the airport that went on for two hours

_____

7 a letter that goes on for ten pages

_____

8 a university course that takes three years

_____

9 a prison sentence of ten years

_____

10 a hotel with five stars

_____

11 a speed limit of 30 miles an hour

_____

12 a house that was built two hundred years ago

_____

# Prepositions

## 11 Adjective + preposition

Complete these sentences with the correct preposition.

1 Are you afraid _____ the dark?

2 She was angry _____ me _____ not telling her the news.

3 Canterbury is famous _____ its cathedral.

4 Bill is jealous _____ me because I'm cleverer than him.

5 I'm very proud _____ my two daughters.

6 I'm disappointed _____ you. I thought I could trust you.

7 You're very different _____ your brother.
  I thought you'd be similar _____ each other.

8 Are you excited _____ going on holiday?

9 Visitors to Britain aren't used _____ driving on the left.

10 Visitors to hot countries need to be aware _____ the risk of malaria.

11 You should be ashamed _____ what you did.

12 I am most grateful _____ all your help.

13 Who is responsible _____ this mess?

14 What's wrong _____ you? You don't look well.

15 My son is crazy _____ a rock group called *The Hives*.

# Pronunciation

## 12 Silent consonants

1 English words often have silent consonants:

kno~~w~~    ~~w~~rite~~r~~    wa~~l~~k    clim~~b~~

**T 8.3** Complete the table with these words. Cross out the silent consonants.

| | | | |
|---|---|---|---|
| ~~industry~~ | executive | ~~honest~~ | inhabitant |
| receipt | distinctly | rebuilt | fasten |
| eccentric | insect | lamp | sumptuous |
| exhausted | whistle | straight | anonymous |
| citizen | fascinating | delighted | documentary |
| landscape | temperature | business | debt |

| A<br>all consonants pronounced | B<br>some consonants not pronounced |
|---|---|
| industry | ~~h~~onest |
| | |

2 **T 8.4** Write these words. They all have silent consonants.

1 /saɪən'tɪfɪk/ _____

2 /saɪ'kɒlədʒɪst/ _____

3 /'hænsəm/ _____

4 /rɪ'si:t/ _____

5 /'krɪsməs/ _____

6 /'naɪtmeə/ _____

7 /klaɪm/ _____

8 /'grænfɑ:ðə/ _____

9 /'wenzdeɪ/ _____

10 /kɑ:m/ _____

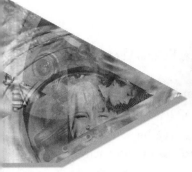

# 9

Expressing habit
*get* and *be*

**Forever friends**

# Present and past habit

▶▶ **Grammar Reference: Student's Book p150**

## 1 Present habit

**1** Match a sentence in **A** with a sentence in **B**.

| A | B |
|---|---|
| 1 ☐ She's really generous. | a He's always applying for new jobs. |
| 2 ☐ He's so disorganized. | b She never thinks before she speaks. |
| 3 ☐ She's very fashionable. | c He won't ever change his mind. |
| 4 ☐ He's so dishonest. | d She's always buying me presents. |
| 5 ☐ She's so sensitive. | e He's always telling lies. |
| 6 ☐ He's really stubborn. | f She'll only wear designer clothes. |
| 7 ☐ She's so rude. | g He never finishes anything he starts. |
| 8 ☐ They're so spoilt. | h She'll start crying at the slightest thing. |
| 9 ☐ She's very energetic. | i They get everything they ask for. |
| 10 ☐ He's very ambitious. | j She jogs to work every day. |

**2** Write more sentences like those in column **B** above. Use either the Present Simple, *always* + Present Continuous, or *will*.

1 She's very fussy about her food. **She never eats anything you make for her.**

2 He's really arrogant. _____

3 She adores ice-cream. _____

4 He hates all sport. _____

5 They're shopping mad. _____

6 He's a real computer nerd. _____

7 She's a telly addict! _____

8 He's really easy-going. _____

9 Their children are very rude. _____

10 He's very kind. _____

## 2 Past habit

**1** Complete the sentences with the correct form of *used to*: positive, question, or negative.

1 There _____ be a beautiful old building where that car park is now.

2 _____ have a Saturday job when you were at school?

3 She _____ be so moody. It's only since she lost her job.

4 _____ play cricket when you were at school?

5 My grandfather never _____ get so out of breath when he climbed the stairs.

6 Julie _____ be as slim as she is now. She's been dieting.

7 Where _____ go out to eat when you lived in Madrid?

8 _____ smoke 60 cigarettes a day? How did you give up?

**2** Which of the verb forms can complete the sentences below? Tick (✔) all possible answers.

1 I _____ long blonde hair when I was first married.
   a ✔ had   b ✔ used to have   c ☐ would have

2 We _____ Auntie Jean every time we went to London.
   a ☐ visited   b ☐ used to visit   c ☐ would visit

3 Pam _____ out with Andy for six months but then she ditched him.
   a ☐ went   b ☐ used to go   c ☐ would go

4 We _____ coffee and croissants every morning for breakfast.
   a ☐ had   b ☐ used to have   c ☐ would have

5 We _____ to each other every day when we were apart.
   a ☐ wrote   b ☐ used to write   c ☐ would write

6 He _____ to me for 25 years and then stopped.
   a ☐ wrote   b ☐ used to write   c ☐ would write

7 In the old days people _____ you if you were in trouble.
   a ☐ helped   b ☐ used to help   c ☐ would help

8 I _____ living so close to the sea.
   a ☐ loved   b ☐ used to love   c ☐ would love

9 Dave _____ Molly three times if she wanted to go out with him.
   a ☐ asked   b ☐ used to ask   c ☐ would ask

10 I _____ questions in class. I was too shy.
   a ☐ never asked   b ☐ never used to ask   c ☐ would never ask

**3** Annoying behaviour

**1** Tick (✔) the sentences where the speaker is annoyed by someone's behaviour.

1 ☐ He watches all the sports programmes on TV.
2 ☐ He's always watching sports programmes on TV.
3 ☐ She'd give us extra lessons after school.
4 ☐ She *would* give us extra lessons after school.
5 ☐ She was always giving us extra lessons.
6 ☐ She used to give us extra lessons.
7 ☐ The cat always sleeps on my bed.
8 ☐ The cat *will* sleep on my bed.
9 ☐ The cat's always sleeping on my bed.

**2** Rewrite the sentences so that they express a criticism.

## My family's bad habits

1 My dad mends his motorbike in the living room.
   _____
   _____

2 My brother leaves the top off the toothpaste.
   _____
   _____

3 My sister often borrows my clothes without asking.
   _____
   _____

4 Uncle Tom smokes cigars in the kitchen.
   _____
   _____

5 My grandpa used to eat toast in bed.
   _____
   _____

6 My grandma didn't use to turn on her hearing aid.
   _____
   _____

## 4 get and be

> **1** Compare these sentences.
>
> Don't worry. You'll soon **get used to** working such long hours.
> I **am used to** working long hours, I've done it for years.
>
> He eventually **got used to** the tropical climate, but it took a long time.
> I was born in India so I'**m used to** a hot climate.
>
> **Get used to** means become used to and describes a change of state. *Be used to* describes a state.
>
> **2** **Get** can be used with other past participles and adjectives to describe changes of state.
>
> The sea'**s getting rough**. Let's go back!
> We **got lost** on the mountain.
> We **got married** last week.
>
> **3** **Get** can sometimes be used with an infinitive to talk about a gradual change.
>
> As I **got to know** Paris, I started to like it more and more.
> I'm sure the kids will soon **get to like** each other.
> The change doesn't have to be gradual. It can be sudden.
> She'll be furious if she **gets to hear** about this.

**1** Complete the sentences with *used to*, *be used to*, or *get used to* in the correct form, positive or negative.

1 If you _____ Indian food, this dish might be too spicy for you.

2 I'll never _____ your hair that short. You'll have to grow it again.

3 A  How do you drive in all this traffic?
   B  I _____ it now, so it's OK. But it took me a while to _____ all the cars, lanes, and bad tempers, believe me!

4 Tom didn't like his new school at first, but he eventually _____ it, and made new friends.

5 I _____ jog every morning, but I don't any more. I'm so unfit now.

6 When I was a boy, I _____ like going to piano lessons, so I stopped. Now I'm in my forties, I've started learning again!

7 Sally won't find it easy to go on a diet. She _____ having three spoonfuls of sugar in her tea and coffee!

8 A  I hate my new job!
   B  Give it a chance. You may _____ it after you've been there a bit longer.

9 _____ you _____ watch old Elvis Presley films on the TV when you were young?

10 A  _____ you _____ your new teacher yet? I know you didn't like her much at first.
   B  Well, I have a bit. She's OK, I suppose.

**2** Complete the sentences with *get* or *be* in the correct form and a word or expression from the box.

| better | ready (×2) | dressed | dark | tired | to like |
|--------|-----------|---------|------|-------|---------|
| to know | a pilot | lost | upset | divorced | |

1 I often _____ when I watch the news. Such awful things are happening in the world.

2 A  How are you feeling?
   B  I _____ slowly, but I still feel weak.

3 My little nephew is determined _____ when he grows up.

4 A  Come on, Helen! The play starts in half an hour.
   B  I _____ in two minutes. I _____ just _____ and putting my shoes on.
   A  I don't know why it takes you so long. I _____ since 6.00.

5 A  Do we turn right or left at the next junction?
   B  I've no idea! I think we _____ .

6 A  Did you hear that Sue and Chris _____ ?
   B  No! I always thought they were the perfect couple.

7 I didn't use to like Mick at all, but the more I _____ him, the more I _____ him. Now he's my best friend!

8 Can we stop walking for a minute? I need a rest. I _____ .

9 In summer it is still light at 9.00 in the evening, but in winter it _____ at 5.00.

## 5 My first love

**1** **T 9.1** Read Geraldine Cook's story.
Which of the verbs in italics …

a … can change to both *used to* or *would*?

b … must stay in the Past Simple?

Put the correct letter a or b next to the verbs.

### ~ *My first love* ~

by novelist GERALDINE COOK

#### I'd be locked in my room to stop me from seeing Jim

I was 14 when I met Jim. One day I (1) ___ *looked up* and saw this tall, slim 19-year-old with blonde hair walking towards me. That minute I (2) ___ *fell* hopelessly in love. From then on, I regularly (3) ___ *waited* on the path when he (4) ___ *passed by* on his way home from work. I (5) ___ *watched* him walk across the fields. He (6) ___ *wore* his coat thrown over one shoulder and his shirt open at the neck. My heart (7) ___ *beat* faster each time I caught sight of him.

At first he (8) ___ *was* tense and worried. Then he (9) ___ *learned* to tolerate me, and after that, every time he saw me, he (10) ___ *smiled and walked quicker*. But nothing else happened. We (11) ___ *were* both very aware of the fact that I (12) ___ *was* not quite 15.

However, my stepfather (13) ___ *found out* and was furious. But I (14) ___ *refused* to stop seeing Jim. So he (15) ___ *locked* me in my bedroom every afternoon for weeks on end. Jim (16) ___ *drove* past my window every day. I (17) ___ *cried* with frustration, because Jim never (18) ___ *saw* me waving at the window. I (19) ___ *worried* that he thought that I (20) ___ *didn't want* to see him any more. Eventually my stepfather (21) ___ *let* me out. And of course I (22) ___ *ran* to find Jim. He (23) ___ *was thrilled* to see me and (24) ___ *asked* me to marry him!

So my stepfather (25) ___ *threw* me out of the house, but Jim's family (26) ___ *took* me home. Most evenings for the next year we (27) ___ *talked about and planned* our wedding. We (28) ___ *got married* on Easter Saturday just after my sixteenth birthday, and after more than 30 years we are still very much in love.

**2** Complete these sentences about the story with one suitable word from the box.

| got wasn't used been would |

1 Geraldine _____ to wait for Jim as he came home after work.

2 Her heart _____ beat faster every time she saw him.

3 Jim wasn't _____ to speaking to 14-year-old girls.

4 Jim eventually _____ used to seeing Geraldine every day.

5 Her stepfather never _____ used to the fact that she was meeting Jim.

6 He _____ used to being disobeyed.

7 Geraldine quickly _____ used to living with Jim's family.

8 Geraldine and Jim _____ talk about getting married for hours on end.

9 They have _____ happily married for over 30 years.

# Vocabulary

## 6 Homonyms

Use the same word to complete each pair of sentences.

1   a   The sun **rose** brightly over the house this morning.

    b   He's very romantic. He always gives me a red **rose** when we go on a date.

2   a   Look out of the window, Josie – there's Daddy coming up the path! _____ to him!

    b   With each huge _____ , the boat was thrown about more and more, and I began to feel really sick.

3   a   Look, I've no idea what you're arguing about. What _____ are you trying to make?

    b   He couldn't speak the language, so he just used to _____ at things in shops when he was buying food.

4   a   Everyone has the _____ to a fair trial.

    b   Well done! You got all the answers _____ in the test.

5   a   Gosh, you look smart! Is that a new _____ and tie you're wearing?

    b   Well, I think you should buy the pale green dress. The red one doesn't _____ you.

6   a   See the man with blue eyes and _____ hair? That's Jenny's husband.

    b   It's not _____ ! You gave him more than me!

7   a   Dave's OK, but he's not really my _____ of guy.

    b   You'll have to speak to him yourself. I can't _____ out all your problems for you.

8   a   Oh, look! Jamie Cullam's on at the Palladium. Can we get tickets? I'm a real _____ of his.

    b   It's boiling hot. Could we switch the _____ on and get some cool air in here?

9   a   She'll be arriving on the 2.30 _____ . Let's go to the station and meet her.

    b   Oh, you're a champion swimmer, are you? How many hours a week do you have to _____ ?

## 7 Homophones

Write the correct spelling of the words in phonetics.

1   a   I'm /bɔːd/! I can't think of anything to do.

    b   He jumped on his surf /bɔːd/ and paddled out to the biggest waves.

      a _____    b _____

2   a   Stop it! You know you aren't /əlaʊd/ to do that!

    b   Jack, can you stand up and read your story /əlaʊd/ to the whole class, please.

      a _____    b _____

3   a   While we were in Alaska, we did some /weɪl/ watching. It was really exciting to see the huge creatures.

    b   When she saw her bag had been stolen, she let out a /weɪl/ and started crying.

      a _____    b _____

4   a   She was happy to get her bag back when the police /kɔːt/ the thief.

    b   The thief was sentenced to three months in prison at /kɔːt/ the next day.

      a _____    b _____

5   a   I need to arrange a /ləʊn/ with my bank manager to pay off my debts.

    b   The bad weather prevented us from climbing any further, but we could see one /ləʊn/ climber on the summit.

      a _____    b _____

6   a   We looked for a car /haɪə/ place in our holiday resort so that we could travel around a bit.

    b   Throw the ball /haɪə/ or you'll never get it in the basket!

      a _____    b _____

*Q   Why is Sunday the strongest day?*
*A   Because all the others are weak days.*

**Patient**  Doctor, I keep thinking I'm a billiard ball.
**Doctor**  Go to the end of the cue.

CUSTOMER  Waiter! What sort of soup is this?
WAITER  It's bean soup, sir.
CUSTOMER  I don't care what it's been. I want to know what it is now.

## Phrasal verbs

### 8 Phrasal verbs and nouns that go together

1 Some phrasal verbs have a strong association with certain objects: *set out on a journey*; *work out the solution to a problem*.

Match a verb with an object. There may be more than one answer, but there is one that is best.

| | | | |
|---|---|---|---|
| 1 ☐ come up with | a someone you respect |
| 2 ☐ break into | b a naughty child |
| 3 ☐ break off | c a problem, a complaint, a difficult customer |
| 4 ☐ tell off | d the other people in the group |
| 5 ☐ bring up | e a university course after one year |
| 6 ☐ count on | f a solution to a problem |
| 7 ☐ deal with | g your best friend to help you |
| 8 ☐ drop out of | h children to be honest and hard-working |
| 9 ☐ fit in with | i a house, a flat, to steal something |
| 10 ☐ look up to | j a fact that someone might not be aware of |
| 11 ☐ point out | k what I said – I didn't mean it |
| 12 ☐ take back | l a relationship, an engagement |

2 Complete the sentences with the correct form of a phrasal verb from exercise 1.

1 The thieves _____ the warehouse and stole goods worth £20,000.

2 He _____ his elder sister, because she always seemed so wise and experienced.

3 I accused you of being mean the other day. I _____ it all _____ . I'm sorry.

4 I hadn't noticed that the living room was a different colour until someone _____ it _____ to me.

5 Scientists will have to _____ new methods of increasing the world's food supply.

6 She _____ Tom _____ because he hit his sister.

7 You have a problem with your order, madam? I'll just get someone to _____ it for you.

8 I had a new student today. He seems very nice. I'm sure he'll _____ the rest of the class just fine.

9 Why did you _____ university after just one term? What are you going to do now?

10 I'm running for President. I hope I can _____ your support.

11 My parents _____ me _____ to finish all the food on my plate.

12 Charles is miserable. Penelope _____ their engagement last week for some reason.

## Listening

### 9 A small disagreement

1 **T 9.2** Listen to the conversation and choose the best answers to these questions.

1 What are the people arguing about?
   a ☐ Nick doesn't want Fiona to watch *Friends* on TV.
   b ☐ Fiona thinks Nick's TV detective programmes are rubbish.
   c ☐ Nick and Fiona can't agree on which TV programmes to watch these days.

2 How do they resolve their disagreement?
   a ☐ They're going to watch *Inspector Morse* together.
   b ☐ They are going to rent more video and DVD films together.
   c ☐ Nick is going to watch *Friends* with Fiona.

2 Tick (✓) the phrases you hear for making a point.

| | |
|---|---|
| 1 ☐ | The point is that … |
| 2 ☐ | If you want my opinion … |
| 3 ☐ | Another thing is that … |
| 4 ☐ | To tell you the truth … |
| 5 ☐ | As far as I'm concerned … |
| 6 ☐ | If you ask me … |
| 7 ☐ | That's not the point … |
| 8 ☐ | The point I'm trying to make is that … |
| 9 ☐ | I suppose the problem is that … |
| 10 ☐ | But the main point is that … |

3 Look at the tapescript on p84 and check your answers.

# Pronunciation

## 10 Weak and strong forms

 **T 9.3** Auxiliary verbs have weak and strong forms, depending on whether they are stressed or unstressed.

1 Sometimes the weak form is a contraction.

| | | |
|---|---|---|
| he is | = | he's |
| she does not | = | she doesn't |
| I have not | = | I haven't |

2 Sometimes the weak form is a change in the vowel sound. This is often a change to /ə/.

| | Weak | Strong |
|---|---|---|
| was | /wəz/ <br> *Was Tom there?* | /wɒz/ <br> *Yes, he was.* |
| were | /wə/ <br> *Were you there?* | /wɜ:/ <br> *Yes, we were.* |
| can | /kən/ <br> *Can you swim?* | /kæn/ (can't = /kɑ:nt/) <br> *Yes, I can.* |
| been | /bɪn/ <br> *I've been shopping.* | /bi:n/ <br> *Where have you been?* |

Some prepositions also have weak and strong vowel sounds.

| | Weak | Strong | | Weak | Strong |
|---|---|---|---|---|---|
| to | /tə/ | /tu:/ | for | /fə/ | /fɔ:/ |
| of | /əv/ | /ɒv/ | from | /frəm/ | /frɒm/ |
| at | /ət/ | /æt/ | | | |

**1** **T 9.4** Circle all auxiliaries and prepositions with weak vowel sounds. Underline all those with strong vowels.

1 I don't want to see him but I'm sure you want to.
2 She isn't going to learn from this experience, but he is.
3 I've heard that you're thinking of moving from London. Are you?
4 They have dinner at seven, don't they?
5 You'll be able to get a ticket for me, won't you?
6 I've got no idea who this letter's from.
7 Can't you remember who Bill used to work for?
8 I've been waiting for you to come. Where were you?
9 We'd been looking forward to coming for ages, then at the last minute we weren't able to.
10 Won't you sit down for a couple of minutes?

**2** **T 9.5** Read the telephone conversation between two friends and transcribe **A**'s lines. Add punctuation to make the meaning clear.

**A** /wɒt ə jʊ du:ɪŋ ət ðə wi:kend/ ?
_____

**B** I haven't decided yet.
**A** /wɪə gəʊɪŋ tə skɒtlənd djʊ wɒnə kʌm tu:/ ?
_____
_____

**B** I'd love to. Where are you staying?
**A** /wiv dɪsaɪdɪd tə kæmp nʌn əv ʌs kən əfɔ:d tə peɪ fərə həʊtel/
_____
_____

**B** Camping in Scotland in October! You'll be freezing cold.
**A** /nəʊ wi wəʊnt wiv gɒt strɒŋ tents lɒts əv wɔ:m kləʊz ən θɪk sli:pɪŋ bægz/
_____
_____

**B** Have you checked the weather forecast?
**A** /əv kɔ:s wi hæv ənd ɪts prɪti wɔ:m fər ɒktəʊbə/
_____

**B** OK then. It'll be quite an adventure!
**A** /eksələnt aɪl tel ðɪ ʌðəz ðeɪl bi dɪlaɪtəd wɪəl pɪk jʊ ʌp ət sɪks ɒn fraɪdeɪ si: jʊ ðen gʊdbaɪ/
_____
_____

**B** Bye!

# 10

## Modal auxiliary verbs in the past

**Risking life and limb**

## Revision of modals

▶▶ **Grammar Reference: Student's Book p151**

### 1 Present to past

Rewrite the sentences to make them refer to the past.

1  I must post the letters.

   **I had to post the letters.**

2  I have to take the pills three times a day.

   _____

   _____

3  They must be away on holiday.

   _____

4  We can't see the top of the mountain.

   _____

   _____

5  He can't be a millionaire.

   _____

6  We mustn't shout in the classroom.

   _____

   _____

7  He won't go to bed.

   _____

8  That will be John on the phone.

   _____

9  You should be more careful.

   _____

10 You could help with the washing-up for a change.

   _____

   _____

## Modal verbs of probability

### 2 How certain?

1  **T 10.1** Decide on the degree of certainty in these sentences. Put two ticks (✓✓) if the idea expressed is certain. Put one tick (✓) if it is less certain.

   1  [✓✓]  You must have seen him at the cinema. I know he was there.
   2  [✓]  The dog is really dirty. He might have swum in the lake.
   3  [  ]  He can't have been telling the truth.
   4  [  ]  He might have left a message on your mobile.
   5  [  ]  I don't know where she is. She may have gone shopping.
   6  [  ]  She must have been very upset when you told her the news.
   7  [  ]  They're not answering their phone. They must have gone away already.
   8  [  ]  I don't see their car. They can't have come back yet.
   9  [  ]  It's six o'clock. Tom will have gone home by now.
   10 [  ]  Matthew isn't here – he might have thought you weren't coming and gone to the cinema by himself.
   11 [  ]  I could have cancelled the meeting if I'd known earlier!
   12 [  ]  Ian'll be back soon. It's Friday. He'll have gone to the pub after work.

2  Make sentences from the table.

| If I go to India, I<br>If I went to India, I<br>If I'd gone to India, I | can<br>will<br>may<br>might<br>would<br>could | see the Taj Mahal.<br><br>have seen the Taj Mahal. |
|---|---|---|

1  _____
2  _____
3  _____
4  _____
5  _____
6  _____

## 3 Past probability

**1** Write sentences for the situations below, using the information in the box.

| | | cut it | a cake. |
|---|---|---|---|
| He | must have | gone | a party last night. |
| She | can't have | mislaid | to Andy. |
| They | might have | arrived home | something naughty. |
| | | got engaged | for ages. |
| | | had | without me. |
| | | been doing | by now. |
| | | been making | my number. |

1  Stella's wearing a beautiful diamond ring.

_____

_____

2  Look at the length of the grass in Bill's garden.

_____

_____

3  The children ran away laughing and giggling.

_____

_____

4  There's flour on grandma's nose.

_____

_____

5  Paulo and Geri said they'd wait for me, but I can't see them.

_____

_____

6  Klaus's flat is so clean and tidy.

_____

_____

7  It's after midnight. Henri and Sally left ages ago.

_____

_____

8  I don't know why Tara didn't ring.

_____

_____

**2** Write sentences for the situations below using the information in the box in the perfect infinitive passive.

| | | watered | by the wind. |
|---|---|---|---|
| It | must have been | washed | by a stone. |
| They | can't have been | hit | properly. |
| | | blown down | recently. |
| | | repaired | while we were away. |
| | | dry-cleaned | with something red. |

1  A tree has fallen across the road.

_____

_____

2  My white jeans have turned pink!

_____

_____

3  My TV has broken and I've only just had it fixed.

_____

_____

4  David's suit looks a bit dirty now.

_____

_____

5  All the flowers in the garden have died.

_____

_____

6  The car windscreen is broken.

_____

_____

"SOMEONE MUST HAVE PLANTED THEM THERE."

## 4 Past modals of deduction

Complete the conversations with the correct form of the verbs in brackets.

1 **A** I wonder how the thief got into our apartment?

**B** He (1) _____ (could / use) the fire escape or he (2) _____ (might / climb up) that tree.

**A** Well he (3) _____ (need not / bother). There's nothing to steal!

2 **A** Bill told me that he'd spent £2,000 on a birthday present for his girlfriend, but he (4) _____ (must / joke). Surely he (5) _____ (can not / spend) that much.

**B** I think you (6) _____ (might / mishear) him!

3 **A** It's three thirty. Mum and Dad's plane landed over an hour ago. They (7) _____ (should / phone)!

**B** They (8) _____ (may / be delayed). No, look! They're driving up now. You (9) _____ (need not / worry).

4 **A** You're very sunburnt. You (10) _____ (should not / burn) if you'd used your factor 30 suncream.

**B** I (11) _____ (must / fall) asleep. And I (12) _____ (can not / put on) enough cream. Ouch!

## 5 Past modals – various uses

Choose the correct answer.

1 I'm sorry. I *shouldn't have / couldn't have* told Tom what you said about him.

2 **A** Where's the dog?

**B** Don't know. Dad *may have / 'll have* taken him for a walk.

**A** No. I remember. It's Tuesday, isn't it? Mum *should have / 'll have* taken him to the vet.

3 **A** Are Pat and Jan definitely coming? I*'d have / might have* thought they'd have arrived by now.

**B** They *should have / could have* been held up by traffic, don't you think?

**A** Or they *might have / needn't have* had an accident!

**B** Don't be silly. Anyway, we*'d have / must have* heard by now if something like that had happened.

**A** Well, I *needn't have / mustn't have* prepared lunch so early. And I think they *should have / may have* rung if they knew they were going to be late.

4 **A** Who was that man?

**B** He *can't have / must have* been a friend of Jane's. He was asking if I'd seen her.

# The Famous Four

## Friends and their dog rescue fall victim in the nick of time

## 6 The Famous Four

1 Read the article and choose the correct answers.

1 The article is called 'The Famous Four' because

a ☐ the children are now famous after rescuing the woman.

b ☐ the children are similar to another group of children in an adventure story.

2 Mrs Hauton, the injured woman, had been in the woods for

a ☐ twenty-four hours.

b ☐ two nights.

3 In hospital, Mrs Hauton

a ☐ recognized and thanked the children.

b ☐ had difficulty remembering the accident.

2 Complete the article putting the modals and verbs in brackets in the past. Sometimes you need to use the continuous infinitive.

I'm sure that the fictional Famous Five, invented by children's story writer Enid Blyton, (1) _____ (will / be) proud of these three children and their dog.

The three young friends were walking their dog in the woods when they saw a hand mysteriously poking through the undergrowth, and decided to investigate. Alison Bailey, 15, her brother Simon, and his friend Liam Stone, both 11, followed Chelsea the dog into the bushes and found an injured woman. She (2) _____ (must / lie) there for more than a day.

Yesterday, paramedics praised the children for saving Mrs Hauton's life. They said she (3) _____ (can not / survive) another night outside.

It is believed that Mrs Hauton (4) _____ (may / have) an epileptic fit while out for a walk last Wednesday. She then (5) _____ (must / fall) and slipped down the bank.

Alison said: 'The lady (6) _____ (can / hear) us and reached her hand out. But she could hardly speak and she was shaking. She (7) _____ (will / get) very cold overnight. She kept repeating that she wanted to get up, but I said that she should stay still because she (8) _____ (can / break) her back. I kept talking to her until the ambulance arrived. I (9) _____ (must / talk) non-stop for at least half an hour!'

Simon and Liam added: 'We were scared stiff at first, but we (10) _____ (need not / be). Then we ran to call an ambulance. We're glad we helped. She (11) _____ (might / die).'

In true Enid Blyton style, the three rescuers have been to hospital to see Mrs Hauton, who is indeed recovering from back injuries and hypothermia. Alison said: 'We popped in to see the lady at the weekend. She still wasn't sure why she was in hospital. She (12) _____ (must / be) very confused when she woke up. She looked a lot better, though.'

Ambulanceman Gary Smart said: 'The children were very quick-thinking. They did everything exactly as they (13) _____ (should / do). And if Mrs Hauton had spent any more time in the woods, it (14) _____ (can / be) fatal.' ∎

# Vocabulary

## 7 Revision: body idioms

**T 10.2** Complete the conversation with the correct form of body idioms from the box.

| | | | |
|---|---|---|---|
| head for business | give her a hand | face the fact | heart-to-heart |
| heart of gold | hands full | heart | sharp tongue |
| put a brave face | pull my leg | | |

**A** How's your little sister getting on with your parents these days? Better?

**B** Yes, a lot better. They had a big (1) _____ talk at the weekend, and that helped.

**A** So what was the problem then?

**B** Well, for one thing, since I moved into my own flat I've had my (2) _____ with sorting it all out, so I haven't been home. My sister's having to (3) _____ that she's the only child left at home now! Also, my parents wanted her to go to university. She tried, but her (4) _____ wasn't in it. She wants to open her own shop.

**A** Yes, she's got a very good (5) _____ , hasn't she?

**B** Yes, she's always been good with money. Anyway, she told my parents that they had to stop trying to run her life for her.

**A** Oh dear! Your poor parents. She's always had a bit of a (6) _____ , hasn't she?

**B** Yes, but she doesn't really mean it. Underneath she has a (7) _____ . She's very kind really.

**A** Oh, I know. But how did your parents react?

**B** Well, I think they (8) _____ on it, but they were really hurt. Anyway, she apologized. And now – guess what? They're all going into business together!

**A** What? I don't believe it. You're (9) _____ !

**B** No, it's true! Her shop opens in three months and my parents are going to (10) _____ with running it.

**A** That's great!

## 8 Physical appearance or personality?

**1** Write these adjectives in the correct columns. Careful! One adjective can go in both columns.

| | | |
|---|---|---|
| moody | big-headed | brainy |
| graceful | wrinkled | quick-thinking |
| skinny | nosy | bald |
| cheeky | well-built | narrow-minded |
| affectionate | smart | curly |
| hard-hearted | | |

| Physical appearance | Personality |
|---|---|
| | |
| | |
| | |
| | |

**2** Complete the sentences with the parts of the body in the box, used as *verbs*.

arm  elbow  eye  foot  hand  head  shoulder  thumb

1 The teacher _____ out the exam papers and told the class to begin writing.

2 I managed to _____ my way to the front of the crowd, so I got a good view of the procession.

3 I haven't read the magazine yet, I just _____ through it to see if there were any interesting pictures.

4 We all _____ the new member of class with curiosity. We were eager to see what she was like.

5 They ordered the most expensive things on the menu because they knew that I _____ the bill.

6 In the final seconds of the match Benson _____ the ball into the back of the net, making it one–nil.

7 Policemen _____ with guns in some countries.

8 I'd hate to be Prime Minister. I don't think I could _____ the responsibility of making so many important decisions.

# Prepositions

## 9 Verb + preposition

Complete the sentences with a verb in its correct form and a preposition.

| Verbs | | Prepositions | |
|---|---|---|---|
| ~~thank~~ | forgive | into | of |
| accuse | hide | at | on |
| trick | hold | for | to |
| congratulate | inherit | from | |
| shout | model | | |
| invite | remind | | |

1 He **thanked** the nurse **for** all her help.

2 You _____ me so much _____ your father. You look just like him.

3 Everyone _____ me _____ passing my driving test at the fourth attempt.

4 My teenage daughter always _____ herself _____ her latest pop idol. She's had a ring put through her nose, just like him.

5 Don't _____ the truth _____ me. I want to know everything.

6 He picked up the crying baby and _____ her tightly _____ his chest.

7 We've _____ 300 guests _____ our wedding.

8 I think that TV ads _____ people _____ buying things that they don't really want.

9 I didn't _____ a penny _____ my great uncle when he died.

10 The spectators _____ abuse _____ the referee when he disallowed the goal.

11 How can I ever _____ him _____ telling me all those lies?

12 I _____ by my employers _____ stealing, which I strongly denied.

# Pronunciation

## 10 Rhymes and limericks

1 **T 10.3** Make rhyming pairs with the words from the box.

| ~~good~~ | chief | court | deaf | fool | mud |
|---|---|---|---|---|---|
| height | lose | knew | knows | grieve | put |
| reign | nude | said | pour | weight | wool |

| should | /ʊd/ | **good** | food | /u:d/ | _____ |
|---|---|---|---|---|---|
| bread | /ed/ | _____ | leaf | /i:f/ | _____ |
| choose | /u:z/ | _____ | taught | /ɔ:t/ | _____ |
| toes | /əʊz/ | _____ | chef | /ef/ | _____ |
| hate | /eɪt/ | _____ | through | /u:/ | _____ |
| tight | /aɪt/ | _____ | wore | /ɔ:/ | _____ |
| full | /ʊl/ | _____ | brain | /eɪn/ | _____ |
| pool | /u:l/ | _____ | leave | /i:v/ | _____ |
| blood | /ʌd/ | _____ | foot | /ʊt/ | _____ |

2 **T 10.4** Limericks are short poems with a distinctive rhythm. The lines rhyme AABBA. Transcribe the lines written in phonetics in these two limericks.

### the PELICAN

A rare old bird is a pelican
His /bi:k kən həʊld mɔ: ðən ɪz beli kən/

_____

He /kən teɪk ɪn hɪz bi:k/

_____

/ɪnʌf fu:d fər ə wi:k/

_____

And I'm damned if I know how the hell he can!

### The Lady from Twickenham

There was a young lady from Twickenham
Whose /ʃu:z wə tu: taɪt tə wɔ:k kwɪk ɪn ðəm/

_____

She came back from a walk
/lʊkɪŋ waɪtə ðən tʃɔ:k/

_____

And she /tʊk ðəm bəʊθ ɒf ənd wəz sɪk ɪn ðəm/

_____

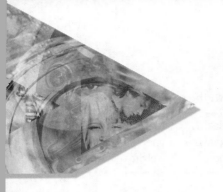

# 11

Hypothesis
*unless, supposing, in case ...*

**In your dreams**

## Real time or unreal time?

▶▶ **Grammar Reference: Student's Book p151**

### 1 Real or hypothetical past?

1 These sentences all have verbs in the Past Simple. Tick (✓) those that refer to real past time. What do the others refer to?

1 ☐ Did you see Lorenzo when you were in Italy?
2 ☐ I wish I worked in the open air.
3 ☐ If you didn't smoke, you wouldn't cough so much.
4 ☐ When we lived in London we'd always travel by bus.
5 ☐ I'd rather we lived in a small country town.
6 ☐ It's time we had a new car.
7 ☐ If only you were always as happy as you are today.
8 ☐ Why didn't you come to the party?

2 These sentences all have verbs in the Past Perfect. Tick (✓) those that express reality and cross (✗) those which don't.

1 ☐ I wish I'd said that.
2 ☐ She asked me if I had known him for a long time.
3 ☐ If I hadn't been so nervous, I would have passed the exam.
4 ☐ If only you'd arrived five minutes earlier.
5 ☐ I woke up and realized it had all been a terrible dream.
6 ☐ What if they hadn't agreed to give you a pay rise?
7 ☐ Had the water risen a bit more, our house would have been flooded.
8 ☐ She told me she'd been given a car for her birthday.

3 Complete the sentences with an auxiliary verb which expresses reality.

1 I wish you didn't bite your nails, but you <u>**do**</u>.
2 I wish I earned more, but I _____ .
3 I should have listened to their advice, but I _____ .
4 If only I could speak Spanish, but I _____ .
5 If only he weren't so selfish, but he _____ .
6 I wish my car would start, but it _____ .
7 I wish you didn't argue all the time, but you _____ .
8 If only I hadn't been fired, but I _____ .
9 I wish I had a flat of my own, but I _____ .

## Wishes and regrets

### 2 Present and past wishes

1 Use the words from the columns to make as many correct and logical sentences as you can.

| I wish | you<br>I | were<br>could<br>would<br>had | come.<br>rich. |
|--------|----------|-------------------------------|----------------|

_____

_____

_____

_____

_____

_____

2 Choose the correct alternative in the following sentences. Sometimes two are possible.

1 I really wish I *can / could / was able to* speak another language.

2 I wish it *wasn't / wouldn't be / isn't* so cold. I hate the winter.

3 It's time we *have / had / have had* a holiday.

4 Our holiday was a disaster. I'd rather we *didn't go / hadn't gone / weren't going.*

5 The party was brilliant after you left. You should *stay / had stayed / have stayed* longer.

6 I wish you *don't speak / didn't speak / wouldn't speak* so quickly. I can't follow you.

7 What were you doing on that wall? Supposing you*'d had / would have / hadn't had* an accident?

8 She'd rather her grandchildren *live / lived / had lived* nearer. Then she could see them more often.

## 3 Expressions of regret

**1** Rewrite the sentences so they have similar meanings, using the words in brackets.

1 I'm sorry I didn't invite him to the party. (wish)

_____

2 Why weren't you watching the road? (should)

_____

3 I regret saying that to her. (If only)

_____

4 I shouldn't have hit him. (wish)

_____

5 I don't want you to tell her. ('d rather)

_____

6 I don't like it when Meg stays out so late. (wish)

_____

7 I regret I didn't work harder for my exams. (should)

_____

**2** Write sentences to express these people's wishes and regrets. Use the expressions from exercise 1.

1 _____     2 _____

_____       _____

3 _____     4 _____

_____       _____

5 _____     6 _____

_____       _____

## 4 What I wish I'd known …

**T 11.1** Read the article and put one word from the box into each gap.

# What I wish I'd known when I was 20

| have | would | should | wish | only | could |
|------|-------|--------|------|------|-------|

**Annette Newman**, 43, MOTHER AND TEACHER

I (1) _____ I'd realized how much I took my mother for granted at that age. If (2) _____ she (3) _____ have lived to see me with my own children! I'm sure she (4) _____ have said, 'I told you so!', and I would (5) _____ replied, 'Sorry Mum, I (6) _____ have listened to you more! I had no idea that being a mother was such hard work!'

| imagine | could | unless | have |
|---------|-------|--------|------|
| hadn't | wouldn't | had | would |

**Simon Hewitt**, 55, ACCOUNTS MANAGER

I wish I (7) _____ been so painfully shy when I was in my teens and twenties. I (8) _____ go out or do anything (9) _____ I really had to. If only someone (10) _____ have told me that I needed to make myself go out and meet people and that it (11) _____ gradually get easier. I have a nice life now, but (12) _____ I conquered my shyness earlier, (13) _____ the life I could (14) _____ had!

| if | 's | realized | could | had | hadn't |
|----|----|----|----|----|----|

**James Garner**, 31, LANDSCAPE GARDENER

I left school with no qualifications, feeling an academic failure. I wish I (15) _____ known then that I (16) _____ have a decent career in gardening. It (17) _____ time that more young people (18) _____ that success can be achieved without passing exams. And (19) _____ I (20) _____ eventually realized that my love of plants could get me the job of my dreams, I would still be moving from one dead-end job to another.

# Third conditional

## 5 My first crash

**1** **T 11.2** Read the article and complete the story with the words in the box.

| | |
|---|---|
| would have ended up | was coming round |
| came to a sudden stop | It was boring |
| we were having | used to work |
| could see the face | didn't ever talk |
| I could do | was annoyed |

## My first crash

### by Philippa Forrester

'When I was a poor student in Birmingham I (1) _____ in the holidays for spare cash. One year I spent six weeks in the accounts department of a local firm. (2) _____ , but there was a lovely guy working there called John and I had a crush on him.

A friend of mine used to drive me to an out-of-town aerobics class after work, and I remember on this particular day (3) _____ a girlie chat about my crush. She was obviously fascinated by my tale of infatuation because she was momentarily distracted from looking at the road, and she went round the corner a little too wide and crossed to the other side of the road.

Unfortunately for us, another car (4) _____ the corner in the opposite direction. But what made it all particularly bizarre was that I (5) _____ of the other driver – it was John from accounts!

I can remember starting to blush as we sailed straight into the side of his car. We (6) _____ with the sound of breaking glass from our headlights, and we got out, embarrassed, wearing our Lycra aerobics outfits.

What a ridiculous coincidence it all was. But I was secretly thrilled – all (7) _____ was stand with my mouth open and say: 'Oh, look, it's John from accounts!' My friend exchanged insurance details with him and that was that. In a fairytale,

**2** Now complete the sentences about the story, using the verbs in brackets in the third conditional. Careful! Sometimes you need to use the continuous form.

1 If Phillipa **hadn't been** (be) a poor student, she **wouldn't have been working** (work) for six weeks in a local firm.

2 She _____ (meet) John if she _____ (work) in the accounts department.

3 She _____ (can/go) to the aerobics classes if her friend _____ (pick her up) in her car.

4 If she _____ (talk) to her friend, her friend _____ (cross) to the other side of the road.

5 If there _____ (be) a car coming in the opposite direction, they _____ (crash).

6 She _____ (blush) if John from accounts _____ (be) in the other car.

7 If she _____ (go) to an aerobics class, she _____ (wear) her Lycra outfit.

8 John _____ (might/continue) talking to her, if she _____ (crash) into him.

John and I (8) _____ making a date, getting together and driving happily ever after. But he probably thought I looked an idiot in my Lycra outfit because he (9) _____ to me after that.

My friend's car wasn't too badly damaged, but she (10) _____ that it was her fault. However, she also saw the funny side – that a crush had turned into a crash. '

**3** Rearrange the words to make excuses in the third conditional.

1 wouldn't / been / if / ill / hadn't / shellfish / had / I / I / have / the

_____

_____

2 phoned / had / had / if / you / have / time / would / I / the / I

_____

_____

3 if / known / had / I / the jumper / washable / wasn't / wouldn't / I / bought / have / it

_____

_____

4 if / it / own / my / eyes / seen / with / hadn't / I / wouldn't / believed / I / have / it

_____

_____

**4** Complete the second sentence to express the excuse in a different way.

1 I didn't know you had a mobile phone. I didn't contact you.

**If I'd known you had a mobile phone, I could / would have contacted you.**

2 I didn't send you a postcard because I didn't know your address.

If I _____

_____ a postcard.

3 I didn't remember when your birthday was. That's why I didn't buy you a present.

If _____

_____ .

4 I'm sorry I'm late. I forgot to set my alarm clock.

If _____

_____ .

5 I broke the speed limit because I was taking my wife to the hospital.

If _____

_____ .

# All conditionals

## 6 Revision of all conditionals

Put the verb in brackets in the correct tense to form either the first, second, third, or zero conditional. There are also some examples of mixed conditionals.

1 If I still _____ (feel) sick, I _____ (not go) on holiday next weekend.

2 You make such delicious chocolate cakes! If you _____ (sell) them, you _____ (make) a fortune.

3 Hello, Liz. Are you still looking for Pat? If I _____ (see) her, I _____ (tell) her you want to speak to her.

4 If Alice _____ (go) to Exeter University, she _____ (not met) her husband, Andrew.

5 **A** Does she love him?

   **B** Of course she does. If she _____ (not love) him, she _____ (not marry) him.

6 If you _____ (buy) two apples, you _____ (get) one free.

7 **A** What _____ you _____ (do) if you _____ (see) a ghost?

   **B** I _____ (run) away!

8 We're lost. If we _____ (bring) the map with us, we _____ (know) where we are.

9 You were very lucky to catch the fire in time. If you _____ (not have) a smoke alarm fitted, the house _____ (burn down).

10 You were very rude to Max. If I _____ (be) you, I _____ (apologize).

11 Ashley is allergic to cheese. If he _____ (eat) cheese, he _____ (get) an awful rash.

12 We've run out of petrol. If you _____ (listen) to me sometimes instead of being so stubborn, you _____ (hear) me saying that we were getting low. Then we _____ (not be) stuck here.

# Ways of introducing conditionals

1 Conditionals can be introduced in a variety of ways other than with *if*.

**unless**

*Unless* means *except if*.

> *We'll go swimming **unless** it rains.*

> ***Unless** there's a strike, I'll be at work tomorrow.*

**in case**

*In case* means the first action is a precaution: it happens because the second action *might* happen. Compare these two sentences.

> *I'll take my umbrella **in case** it rains.* (I plan to take my umbrella.)

> *I'll take my umbrella **if** it rains.* (I don't plan to take my umbrella if I don't have to.)

**Supposing ... / Suppose ... / Imagine ...**

These mean the same as *Imagine if ...?* or *What if ...?* The condition is more improbable, so they are more often found in second and third conditionals. They are questions, and they come at the beginning of a sentence.

> ***Supposing** you could go on holiday tomorrow, where would you go?*

> ***Imagine** you were rich, what would you buy?*

2 In more formal styles *if* can be dropped and the auxiliary verb inverted.

> ***Were** you to **question** me about the matter, I would deny all knowledge.*

> ***Had** I **known** that he was a journalist, I would have said nothing.*

> ***Should** the meeting **last** longer than expected, I'll have to cancel my dinner engagement.*

'He refuses to come down unless you agree to all of his demands.'

# 7 Words other than *if*

1 Choose the correct word.

1 *In case / Imagine* there were no more wars – wouldn't that be wonderful?
2 I'm going to take a cushion to the concert, *in case / unless* the seats are hard.
3 We'll miss the beginning of the film *should / unless* you hurry.
4 *Unless / In case* you behave yourself, you can't come to the party with us.
5 *Suppose / Should* you got lost, what would you do?
6 I'll take a book *in case / unless* I'm bored on the journey.
7 *Had / Supposing* I understood the problem, I'd have done something about it.
8 *Should / In case* you fail to pay this bill, court action will be taken.

2 Rewrite these sentences using the words in brackets.

1 I won't come if they don't invite me. (unless)

_____

_____

2 What would you do if he left you? (supposing)

_____

_____

3 If you had learned to play tennis, would you have been a champion by now? (suppose)

_____

_____

4 We're going to install a smoke alarm. There may be a fire. (in case)

_____

_____

5 She won't get that job if she doesn't learn to speak French. (unless)

_____

_____

6 If the lifeguard hadn't been there, what would have happened? (imagine)

_____

_____

7 I won't go out this evening. Paul might ring. (in case)

_____

_____

8 I'll be at my desk until 6.00, if you need to speak to me about the matter. (should)

_____

_____

# Vocabulary

## 8 Similar words, different meaning

These adjective pairs are easy to confuse. Complete the sentences with the correct adjectives.

**unreadable** **illegible**

1 I couldn't work out who the letter was from. The signature was completely _____ .

2 I know Shakespeare is very popular but I find him totally _____ .

**childish** **childlike**

3 Sarah is so _____ . She's always having temper tantrums.

4 It was wonderful to watch the lambs playing. I got such _____ pleasure from it.

**sensible** **sensitive**

5 Sophie is extremely _____ at the moment. Anything you say upsets her.

6 Karen is not a very _____ person. She wore high-heeled shoes for our four-mile walk.

**true** **truthful**

7 I've never known her to tell a lie. She's a very _____ person.

8 I can never watch sad films that are based on a _____ story. They always make me cry.

**intolerable** **intolerant**

9 Susan is so _____ of other people. She never accepts anyone else's opinion, and she always thinks she knows best.

10 I find Mark's behaviour _____ . It's unfair to be so selfish.

**economic** **economical**

11 We're having an _____ crisis at the moment. James has lost his job and I don't know how we are going to pay the mortgage.

12 It's much more _____ to drive slowly. You get more kilometres for your money.

# Phrasal verbs

## 9 Nouns from phrasal verbs

 1 There are many nouns formed from phrasal verbs. Sometimes the verb comes first, sometimes second.

*make*-up    *down***fall**    up***bring***ing

*draw*back    *out***break**    *take***away**

2 Sometimes the noun is related to the phrasal verb, and sometimes it isn't.

*I don't use much **make-up**.*

*She **made up** her face very carefully.* = related

*The main **drawback** to your plan is that it's too expensive.* (drawback = disadvantage)

***Draw back** the curtains and let the sunshine in.* (draw back = open)

Complete these sentences with the nouns in the box.

| outcome | breakthrough | outbreak | takeaway |
|---------|--------------|----------|----------|
| check-up | breakdown | comeback | feedback |
| outlook | downfall | | |

1 The _____ of communication between management and workers means the strike will continue.

2 His pop career has suffered recently, but now with a new album and a world tour, he's trying to make a _____ .

3 I go to the dentist twice a year for a _____ .

4 The _____ of the election is that the Labour party has a majority of 90.

5 The weather should be fine over the next few days, and the _____ for the weekend is warm and sunny.

6 There has been an _____ of food poisoning as a result of people eating poorly-cooked chicken.

7 There has been a significant _____ in the search to find a cure for the common cold.

8 Producers ask customers to complete questionnaires because they need _____ to improve their products.

9 We're having a Chinese _____ for supper.

10 He used to be a highly successful pop star, but taking too many drugs was his _____ .

# Listening

## 10 What a pain!

**1** **T 11.3** Listen and answer the questions.

1 What's Mark trying to do?
2 What two things is he having trouble with?
3 What does Greg think is the problem?
4 Why does Mark get upset?
5 Who finds the solution and how?

**2** **T 11.3** Listen again and match these expressions with *if*.

| | |
|---|---|
| 1 I haven't made much progress, | a they'll just have to give you your money back. |
| 2 If you've got a minute, | b if any at all. |
| 3 If the worst comes to the worst, | c that'd be great. |
| 4 Here are your missing parts, | d you might just be finished by then! |
| 5 If all goes well from now on, | e if I'm not mistaken! |

**3** Who says these things, Mark or Greg? Write **M** or **G**.

1 ☐ It's turning into a nightmare already.
2 ☐ What a pain!
3 ☐ Oh, this flatpack stuff is a real pain.
4 ☐ I don't believe it!
5 ☐ This has gone beyond a joke!
6 ☐ It's just that I'm fed up with the whole thing already.
7 ☐ This sort of thing drives me mad, too.
8 ☐ I could kick myself!

**4** Look at the tapescript on p85 and check your answers.

# Pronunciation

## 11 Ways of pronouncing *ea*

**1** There are several different ways of pronouncing the letters *ea*. Look at the examples in the columns below.

| /e/ | /iː/ | /ɪə/ |
|---|---|---|
| bread | meat | fear |
| **/eə/** | **/eɪ/** | **/ɜː/** |
| wear | break | learn |

**2** **T 11.4** Put these words into the correct column according to the pronunciation of *ea*.

| | | | |
|---|---|---|---|
| dear | tear (n) | tear (v) | scream |
| steak | breath | breathe | breadth |
| hear | thread | bear | cheat |
| clear | deaf | death | earth |
| beast | beard | pearl | pear |
| heal | health | great | gear |
| jealous | lead (v) | lead (n) | leap |
| leapt | meant | reason | search |
| swear | theatre | weary | weapon |

# 12

Articles
Determiners

**It's never too late**

## Articles

▶▶ **Grammar Reference: Student's Book p152**

### 1 *a, the*, or zero article?

1 Complete the sentences with *a, the*, or nothing (the zero article).

1 Excuse me! Is there _____ bank near here?

2 **A** I haven't got any money.
  **B** I'm going to _____ bank. I'll get you some.'

3 Has _____ postman been this morning?

4 My brother works as _____ postman.

5 We've seen a house we want to move to. It's got _____ views over fields, and there's _____ lovely garden at _____ back.

6 **A** Where's Nick?
  **B** In _____ garden.'

7 I bought _____ dog to protect myself against _____ burglars.

8 Tony joined _____ the Police Dog Unit because he likes working with _____ dogs.

9 We went out for _____ meal last night. _____ food was excellent. I don't usually like _____ Chinese food, but _____ duck was superb.

2 **T 12.1** Complete the newspaper article with *a, an, the, her*, or nothing.

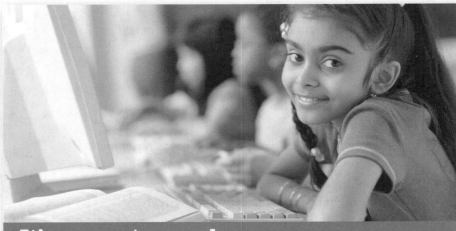

## It's never too early
### Abha, 7, gains her GCSE in computing

(1) _____ girl aged seven went into *The Guinness Book of Records* yesterday when she became (2) _____ youngest pupil ever to pass (3) _____ national exam.

Abha Subramanian's C grade in (4) _____ computer studies was also (5) _____ latest achievement for (6) _____ college run from two rooms of (7) _____ house in Manchester.

Abha earned her place in (8) _____ record books by studying for several evenings (9) _____ week at (10) _____ nearby Ellesmere College.

'I think (11) _____ computers are easy, but I thought (12) _____ exam was quite hard,' Abha said. She praised (13) _____ teacher, James Nolan,

(14) _____ founder and principal of Ellesmere College. 'He is (15) _____ nice teacher – he tells (16) _____ jokes!'

Dr Nolan commented: 'You must have (17) _____ faith in children. They can make (18) _____ paper planes one minute and write (19) _____ computer program (20) _____ next. (21) _____ pupils at my school aren't prodigies – they are just interested and motivated. They are (22) _____ example of what (23) _____ rest of (24) _____ country could be doing.

As far as I'm concerned, students who go to university are the OAPs* of (25) _____ academic world, having passed their mental peak.'

* OAP = an Old Age Pensioner (or, more properly, a Senior Citizen) is a person who has reached retirement age.

# Determiners

▶▶ **Grammar Reference: Student's Book p152**

## 2 *all* and *every*

**1** Choose the correct answer.

1 Anna is such a show-off, she thinks she knows *all/ everything*.

2 My driving test was a complete disaster. *All/Everything* went wrong.

3 Kate didn't say where she was going. *All/Everything* she said was that she was going out.

4 *All/Every* child in the class failed the exam.

5 *All/Everything* I want for my birthday is to lie in bed until midday.

6 I'm starving. *All/Everything* I've eaten today is a packet of crisps.

7 I really don't get on with my new boss. I disagree with *all/everything* she says.

8 I can't go higher than £500 for the car. That's *everything/ all* I can afford.

9 Megan couldn't believe her luck. *All/Every* topic she had revised the night before came up in the exam.

10 The film was so boring that *all/everybody* fell asleep.

**2** Choose the correct answer.

1 I have three dogs. *All/Every* of them love going for a walk, but *neither/none* of them likes being brushed.

2 You can borrow *either/each* the Renault or the Rover. They're *all/both* in the garage.

3 My two daughters are *each/both* good at languages, but *none/neither* of them can do maths at all.

4 I have a shower *every/each* day.

5 I have *any/no* idea how I spend all my money. At the end of *every/either* month, it's all gone.

6 I know *every/each* word of his songs by heart.

7 There are fifteen rooms in this hotel. *Each/Every* room is a little different.

8 You can have *either/each* an orange or an apple, but you can't have *either/both*.

9 **A** Tea or coffee?
   **B** *Either/Neither*, thanks. I've got to rush.

10 **A** Red wine or white?
    **B** *Either/Neither*, whichever is open.

11 I know *either/both* Robert and his brother, but I don't like *both/either* of them.

12 I have four brothers. *Every/Each* of us is different.

# Demonstratives

## 3 *this, that, these, those*

Put *this*, *that*, *these*, or *those* into each gap.

1 _____ shoes are killing me. I can't wait to take them off.

2 (On the phone) Hello. _____ is Beth. Can I speak to Kate?

3 _____ was a wonderful film, wasn't it?

4 I knew Jenny at university. In _____ days she had long blonde hair.

5 **A** Anything else?
   **B** No, _____ 's all for today, thanks.

6 Well, _____ 'll be £5.50, please.

7 I can't get _____ ring off my finger. It's stuck.

8 You just can't get proper sausages _____ days.

9 Come here and tidy up _____ mess right now!

10 Listen to _____ . It says in the paper that life's been found on Mars.

11 Did you ever hear from _____ girl you met on holiday last year?

12 I was in the pub last night when _____ bloke came up to me and hit me.

13 **A** I got a parking fine today.
    **B** _____ 'll teach you a lesson.

14 Who were _____ people you were talking to last night?

15 What was _____ noise? Didn't you hear it?

GEORGE BELIEVES THE WORLD WOULD BE A BETTER PLACE IF **EVERYBODY** WAS AN UNDER-ACHIEVER!

# Revision of articles, determiners, and demonstratives

## 4 Personal column

**T 12.2** Complete the article with the words in the boxes.

### Personal column

# She's a world-travelling, windsurfing OAP who refuses to act her age

## BY SIMON MARTIN

| every | one | her | ~~all of the~~ | the | a | a great deal of |
|---|---|---|---|---|---|---|

ELSIE MORECAMBE looks up at (1) **all of the** large grey clouds coming quickly over (2) _____ horizon. 'I'll go just (3) _____ last time,' she says, jumping onto (4) _____ windsurfing board and speeding off over rough waves.

Back on dry land, (5) _____ group of elderly people watches (6) _____ move of hers with (7) _____ admiration.

| enough | an | the | her | a lot of | a great deal |
|---|---|---|---|---|---|

Four years ago, at 70, looking (8) _____ younger than her years, Elsie formed (9) _____ organization called 'Age Well'. 'It isn't (10) _____ to tell people – you have to show them,' she says, dragging (11) _____ board ashore to (12) _____ back-slapping and praise from (13) _____ group.

| all | her | everything | no | those | their |
|---|---|---|---|---|---|

This is all part of (14) _____ campaign to show that people of (15) _____ ages can achieve (16) _____ they want to do, if they really want to do it. 'It struck me that (17) _____ friends of mine who had (18) _____ job to go to any more and who kept complaining about (19) _____ boring and meaningless lives, didn't have to live like that,' she commented.

| the (× 2) | her (× 2) | this | most | a | several |
|---|---|---|---|---|---|

Elsie has been windsurfing (20) _____ summer months for the last six years, ever since (21) _____ son told her that she was far too old to attempt it. Then she went on (22) _____ solo six-month world trip to Mexico, Thailand, and New Zealand.

Over the last four years she has organized and led (23) _____ groups on trips to Ireland, Israel, and Greece.

So far (24) _____ year she has been walking in (25) _____ Pyrénées, touring on (26) _____ bicycle, and canoeing.

'(27) _____ secret to life is ignoring how old you are,' Elsie says.

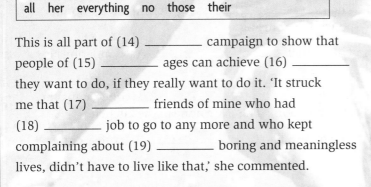

# Nouns in groups

1 There are three main ways that we can put nouns together.

| noun + noun | noun + 's + noun |
|---|---|
| *post office* | *my wife's sister* |
| *headache* | *the doctor's surgery* |
| *face-lift* | *the dog's bowl* |

noun + preposition + noun

*the end of the garden*
*a story about compassion*
*the arrival of the police*

2 Sometimes more than one structure can be used.

*the Prime Minister's arrival*
*the arrival of the Prime Minister*

*the floor of the living room*
*the living room floor*

*the car door handle*
*the handle on the car door*

But usually only one pattern is possible.

*the back of the car*
NOT *the car back*  *the car's back*

3 Sometimes there is a change in meaning.

*the cat's food* = the food that belongs to one particular cat

*The dog has eaten the **cat's food**.*

*cat food* = food for cats in general

*Can you buy some more **cat food** when you go out?*

4 We use the noun + noun pattern (compound nouns) for everyday established combinations. We talk about *a love film*, *a horror film*, but not *a horse film*. Here we usually prefer the pattern with a preposition – *a film about horses*.

THE DOG'S BATH

## 5 Combining nouns

Combine the words in brackets using one of the three patterns. Sometimes there is more than one answer.

1 Your coat's on the _____ (back, chair).

2 You've just spilt the _____ (milk, cat).

3 Can you buy some _____ (paper, toilet)? We've run out.

4 I never listened to my _____ (advice, parents).

5 Can you buy a _____ (wine, bottle) to have with dinner?

6 What did that _____ (road, sign) say? Did you see it?

7 It's such a mess in here. There are empty _____ (wine, bottles) everywhere.

8 The _____ (Prime Minister, duties) include entertaining heads of state.

9 The _____ (my shoe, heel) has come off.

10 Can I borrow your _____ (brush, hair)?

11 What happened at the _____ (film, end)?

12 Here is _____ (today, news).

13 Where is the nearest _____ (Underground, station)?

14 It's my _____ (anniversary, parents, wedding) next week.

15 The _____ (company, success) is due to its efficiency.

16 I've got a _____ (fortnight, holiday) next month.

17 The _____ (government, economic policy) is confusing.

18 The annual _____ (rate, inflation) is about 4%.

19 Are there any _____ (coffee, cups) in your bedroom? There are none in the kitchen.

20 Do you want a _____ (coffee, cup)?

# Vocabulary

## 6 Hot Verbs *be* and *have*

**1** Match the words and expressions with *be* or *have*. Tick the correct column.

| be | | have |
|----|----|----|
| ✓ | fed up with sb/sth | |
| | a right to do sth | ✓ |
| | the nerve to do sth | |
| | on the safe side | |
| | in touch with sb | |
| | a word with sb | |
| | no point in doing sth | |
| | on one's mind | |
| | up to date | |
| | no chance of doing sth | |

**2** Complete the sentences with one of the expressions in the correct form.

1  My job is so boring. I **'m really fed up with** it.

2  If you don't like your meal, you _____ complain to the manager.

3  Thank you for your interview, Miss Clarke. We _____ you as soon as we've made a decision about the job.

4  I can't stop thinking about my ex-girlfriend. She _____ always _____ .

5  Mrs Bennett! Can I _____ you for a minute? It's about your son Ben.

6  Jack was so cheeky! He _____ tell me that this dress didn't suit me!

7  I've got extra holiday insurance just in case. I always like _____ .

8  Well, I'll apply for the manager's job, but I know I _____ getting it.

9  Wait here. If you don't like heights, there's _____ climbing up the tower with us.

10  I got an email from my old friend Suzanne the other day. I _____ her for twenty years now!

# Prepositions revision

## 7 Noun + preposition

Complete the sentences with a preposition or a combination of prepositions.

1  After running up the stairs, I was _____ breath.

2  You make some silly mistakes, but _____ general your work has been good.

3  I went on holiday _____ my own, because sometimes I like to be _____ myself.

4  I got a cheque _____ £500 in the post.

5  There has been a rise _____ the number of violent crimes.

6  The difference _____ you and me is that I don't mind hard work.

7  I can think of no reason _____ her strange behaviour.

8  It took a long time to find a solution _____ the problem.

9  I need some information _____ global warming.

10  I'm having trouble _____ my car. It won't start in the mornings.

11  In the accident there was quite a bit of damage _____ my car.

12  Investigators are trying to find the cause _____ the accident.

13  I've got to do my homework _____ tomorrow.

14  I don't see James any more. I haven't been _____ touch with him for years.

15  Did you get an invitation _____ David's wedding?

*Mr & Mrs John Evans*
*Request the honour of your presence*
*at the marriage of their daughter Rhian Eleri*
*to David Alastair Austin*
*son of Mr & Mrs James Austin*

*at 2.30 p.m. on 13th July 2006 at*
*St George's Church, Newton*
*Swansea*

*~ R.S.V.P. ~*

# Listening

## 8 The holiday of a lifetime

**1** [T 12.3] Listen to Neil and Emma's conversation and mark the questions true (T) or false (F).

1 ☐ Neil wants an adventure holiday.
2 ☐ Emma wants an adventure holiday.
3 ☐ They look in some brochures for some ideas.
4 ☐ Emma wants to go to the Maldives to have sailing lessons.
5 ☐ Neil thinks it'll be expensive.
6 ☐ They decide that it might suit them both.

**2** [T 12.3] Listen again and complete these lines with the correct linking and commenting expression.

1 _____ , windsurfing is very exciting …

2 _____ , I prefer something a bit more relaxing …

3 _____ , we don't get much holiday a year.

4 _____ , we can find something that suits us both.

5 _____ , you weren't paying attention to a thing I was saying!

6 _____ , there'll be sailing lessons, too.

7 _____ , you can bet your life that it'll cost a fortune.

8 _____ , it's not too bad if you go off-season.

**3** Look at the tapescript on p85 and check your answers. Find more linking and commenting expressions.

# Pronunciation

## 9 Nouns and verbs

In the chart the nouns end in an unvoiced sound (/s/, /f/, /θ/), and the verbs end in a voiced sound (/z/, /v/, /ð/).

[T 12.4] Complete the chart with the words and the phonetics. The vowel sound or the spelling changes.

| Noun | | Verb | |
|------|------|------|------|
| advice | | | /ədvaɪz/ |
| | | to use | |
| abuse | | | |
| | /bɪliːf/ | | |
| | | | /rɪliːv/ |
| grief | | | |
| | /ɪkskjuːs/ | | |
| breath | | | |
| | | to halve | |
| | /haʊs/ | | |
| safe | | | |
| | | | /beɪð/ |

## 10 Emphasis in speaking

[T 12.5] Mark where the main stress is in **B**'s replies. Listen, check, and repeat.

1 **A** Why didn't you do your homework last night?
  **B** I <u>did</u> do it.

2 **A** Who made this mark on the carpet?
  **B** I did it. Sorry.

3 **A** Did you know that Johann and Maria are coming tonight?
  **B** I knew Johann was coming.

4 **A** Did you know that Johann and Maria are coming tonight?
  **B** I knew that ages ago.

5 **A** Who told Gran that I crashed her car?
  **B** I didn't tell her.

6 **A** I wish you hadn't told Gran I crashed her car.
  **B** I didn't tell her.

7 **A** I lost all my money playing cards.
  **B** I told you.

8 **A** You don't like Mike and Annie, do you?
  **B** I like Annie.

9 **A** Why don't you like Annie?
  **B** I do like Annie. I think she's great.

10 **A** I feel so sorry for Annie. Nobody likes her.
   **B** I like her.

# Tapescripts

## Unit 1

T 1.5

J  Hi, Mike. I was just passing and I thought I'd drop in. Hope that's OK.

M  Absolutely fine. Nice to see you. Haven't seen you for a while, Jerry! Come on in.

J  Thanks. You're looking well.

M  Thanks! I'm just back from holiday, actually. What about you? What have you been up to lately?

J  Nothing much. Just working hard. That's all.

M  That's a drag. How come you're so busy?

J  I've got a new boss and he's a bit scary. Thinks he's such a big shot. Actually, I'm a bit worried for my job.

M  I don't get it. You've always been so good at your job.

J  Well, that's as maybe, but he really doesn't like me for some reason. Don't know why.

M  What are you going to do? Change jobs?

J  I hope not. I don't feel up to writing endless letters and going to interviews.

M  You need a holiday!

J  You're kidding! Can't afford it. Sara and I are saving up for a new car.

M  That's silly. Holidays are important!

J  I know, but Sara's really fed up with our old car. But maybe you're right. It'd help me to sort things out a bit. OK, I'll talk things over with Sara again, and see if I can't persuade her.

M  Good for you!

J  Cheers, Mike. You're a good mate.

## Unit 2

T 2.5

A  Hey, Sebastian. What a surprise!

S  Hi, Alex. Hi, Marie.

A  Why the long face?

S  Well, I'm just back from a camping trip with Tiffany.

A  Ah! I take it that didn't go very well, then?

S  It was a complete disaster, in fact. I should have realized that she wasn't the camping type when she turned up with like two suitcases and a hairdryer and stuff like that.

A  Whoops!

M  I mean, how silly!

S  Yes, and you should have seen her face when she saw the tent. Don't know what she expected. Some sort of hotel room, probably, in the middle of the field.

A  Oh, dear.

M  What a shame!

S  Yeah, well, she thought so, too! Anyway, it went from bad to worse, because then at night the bad weather set in, and the wind was blowing the tent quite hard, and she sort of started crying a bit, saying that she was scared. And I was trying to like reassure her, and say it wasn't so bad, when all of a sudden the wind really started pulling the tent over …

M  How awful!

A  Oh no!

S  Yeah, maybe Tiffany's right and I do need a new tent! Anyway, I dropped the torch and it all went dark, and she kind of freaked out and started running across the field with her sleeping bag over her head. I mean, how was I to know that she was scared of the dark?

M  Oh, what a nightmare! Poor you!

A  So what happened next? I'm enjoying this.

S  Thanks! Well, I ran after her and fell over into some sort of disgusting muddy stuff …

M  Yuck!

S  … and I started to smell really bad! Anyway, she'd got to the car and refused to move. So I had to go and get all the stuff in the wind and the rain and take it back to the car, and then get in and drive for two hours back home. And the car smelt really awful and we were dirty and soaking wet, and not talking to each other …

M  I can't believe it! What a ridiculous thing to happen!

S  Yes, well, that's what I thought, 'cause when we finally got back home, I thought 'Phew! What a relief!' and then I started to laugh, like really laugh, and I couldn't stop.

A  Uh? So what did she say to that?

S  She was furious! She caught a taxi and went off … still with the sleeping bag round her and grass and leaves in her hair and everything. Don't know what the taxi driver must have thought. Anyway, she phoned me earlier this evening. I'm going there in a minute.

A  Wow. What do you think she's going to say?

S  Can't imagine. I've got some apologizing to do, for a start.

A  What rubbish! None of it was your fault.

M  Shhh, Alex! Let him sort it out himself. Good luck, Sebastian!

A  Yes, and let us know how it all ends. Best story I've heard in ages!

## Unit 3

T 3.5

B  Hey, Mark!

M  Hi, Becky.

B  Did you see that programme last night on Channel 4?

M  No, I didn't.

B  It was this amazing story about a family in the States.

M  Go on, then. Tell me.

B  Well, this girl got pregnant at 17 by this soldier going to the Vietnam war. And in those days you weren't allowed to keep the baby. So she was like sent to a secret home for unmarried mothers, and then the baby was taken from her after the birth.

M  Was it? Poor girl. What happened to the baby's father, then?

B  Actually, when he came home from the war, they got married, anyway, and they had a daughter. But they couldn't find out who had adopted their son, because it'd all been so secret.

M  What a shame! That's awful.

B  And the daughter grew up not knowing she had a brother somewhere. Anyway, the mother kept looking for like twenty years. She and her husband had eventually divorced.

M  Really? Then what happened?

B  Apparently, the father sort of accidentally told his daughter after the divorce that she had a brother. And so she joined in the search for him. Well, by that time the daughter had moved to San Francisco. And she'd made some new friends. And one evening she was round to have dinner with them. And she was introduced to some new people.

M  Don't tell me that …

B  Wait a minute … . I haven't finished yet! She got talking to some guy and she was telling him how sad she was that she couldn't find her adopted brother, and he was saying, yeah, he understood, 'cause like he was adopted and he couldn't find his birth mother, either. And she said she was particularly sad because her brother's birthday was coming up soon on August 9, and he said that his …

**M** I don't believe it …

**B** Yes, that was his birthday, too!

**M** You're kidding! So he was her brother!

**B** Yeah, they had a DNA test to prove it!

**M** Bet the mother was pleased.

**B** Of course. She was over the moon! And she couldn't believe the number of coincidences that had brought them together. First, they both moved to San Francisco. And they both chose the same area to live in, and then they both made the same friends!

**M** That's amazing! What are the chances of that happening?

# Unit 6

**T 6.2**

**A** Good morning, IBM Guilford. How can I help you?

**B** Could you put me through to John Barker, please?

**A** Certainly. … The line's busy. Will you hold?

**B** Yes, that's fine.

**A** Putting you through now.

**B** Thank you.
…

**C** Hello, John Barker.

**B** John? It's Ellen Miles, from Danson Associates.

**C** Ellen! How are things?

**B** Well, I have a problem with an order I placed with you.

**C** How can I help?

**B** You know the delivery of the laptops and powerpoints we discussed a while back? You confirmed the order yourself in writing a fortnight ago.

**C** Oh, yes.

**B** Well, the order hasn't turned up yet, and you did say that delivery would take a week maximum.

**C** Well, yes. It usually does. Let me look up the warehouse schedules. Bear with me a moment.

**B** Of course.

(tap tap tap)

**C** Do you have the order code to hand?

**B** Are you ready? It's FED 20457/80498 MX.

**C** Sorry, didn't quite get the last bit. What was it again?

**B** 80498 MX.

**C** Thanks. I'll read that back to you. FED 20457/80498 MX?

**B** That's right.

**C** And can you confirm the date on the order slip for me, please?

**B** 22nd August.

**C** Well, that all seems to be in order. According to this, the consignment was sent out on September 1.

**B** Well, nothing's arrived.

**C** I'll need to look into it further and get back to you. Are you in the office this afternoon?

**B** Well, I would be normally, but something's come up. I'm here till 12.00.

**C** Then I'll get back to you before 12.00. Don't worry. I'll sort it out.

**B** Thanks, John. I'll expect your call.

# Unit 7

**T 7.2**

**A** What's wrong, Sophie?

**B** Oh, nothing much, Anya.

**A** What do you mean? You look absolutely terrible!

**B** Oh, I'm just a bit upset, that's all.

**A** What about? It's not Charlie again, is it?

**B** Well, yes. He made one or two hurtful remarks this evening.

**A** One or two? He's always criticizing you these days! I don't know how you can stand it!

**B** Well, he's been having a bit of trouble at work recently. So he's quite stressed.

**A** Quite stressed? That's no excuse for being rude to his girlfriend, I don't think. I think his behaviour is totally out of order.

**B** Yeah, it's getting me down a bit, I must say. Well, you really mustn't put up with it any longer, Sophie. You should tell him that if he can't be nicer to you, you won't go out with him any more.

**B** Oh, I suppose so. But the trouble is, I'm really crazy about him, you know.

**A** Well, that's obvious, or you wouldn't put up with all his terrible behaviour …

**B** And he loves me too. I know it.

**A** Well, he's got a funny way of showing it, I must say.

**B** I suppose you're right. Our relationship hasn't been great lately. We haven't been getting on very well.

**A** You're not kidding. You've both been completely miserable. Honestly, Sophie, you must do something about it. It's no good waiting until things get magically better. It isn't going to happen.

**B** OK, OK, Anya. I'll talk to him tonight, I promise.

**A** Good! Now put a smile on your face and let's go and dance!

**B** All right, all right, just let me go and wash my face first. Can't go on the dance floor looking like this.

**A** Well, that's true. You could look a bit better than you do!

**B** Charming, I must say!

**A** That's more like it! You sound loads better already! Come on. Let's go.

# Unit 9

**T 9.2**

**N** What are you watching?

**F** Shh! It's the last ever episode of *Friends*.

**N** Oh, good. It's finishing, then, is it?

**F** Shut up! Talk to you later.
…

**N** Finished now?

**F** Yes, it was great. Ross and Rachel finally got back together.

**N** I don't know how you can watch all that sitcom rubbish.

**F** It isn't rubbish! It's really well written, and very funny.

**N** Well written? How can it be well written when it's written by committee? There are at least 27 writers on these sitcoms.

**F** The point is that only the funniest lines go in. You think it's funny, too. Admit it. You always used to come in the room when it was on and start laughing.

**N** OK. It is quite funny sometimes. But as far as I'm concerned, all these sitcoms are just so trivial. Why do you waste your time on them?

**F** Because they make me laugh, like I said. And as for trivial – if you ask me, they're no more trivial than your rubbish detective programmes. If I try to watch one of those, I'm bored stiff within 20 minutes.

**N** That's because it's got a plot, a storyline, and you can't follow it!

**F** What a cheek! There is no plot. Either it's perfectly obvious within 10 minutes who the murderer is, or the story is so complicated that anybody could have done it! Another thing is that all these detectives are the same character. They're all difficult people to work with, they've all got problems in their private lives, and they always solve the murder case in spite of everybody else saying they're wrong. The point I'm trying to make is that you can't insult my TV viewing habits just because they're different from yours. Yours are no better – just different.

**N** I suppose the problem is that we never watch anything together like we used to. Remember we'd lie on the sofa and watch

Inspector Morse together on Wednesday nights?

**F** Yes, or *24* on a Friday. Well, why don't we get out more videos and DVDs? We used to do that a lot, too. We'd usually find something we both wanted to watch.

**N** Yeah, or we'd take turns to choose. OK, let's do that. We'll start this weekend.

**F** Fine. Now let me tell you what happened in the final episode of *Friends*. You want to know really ...

**N** Oh, all right then. Go on ...

## Unit 11

**T 11.3**

**G** Hello, Mark. I just came to see how you were getting on with setting up your home office. How's it going?

**M** Greg! Come in, come in. Well, I've spent all morning on it, but I haven't made much progress, if any at all.

**G** How come?

**M** Well, I can't get my new computer to work for one thing, and I can't even set up my new computer table. It's turning into a nightmare already.

**G** What a pain! Need any help?

**M** If you've got a minute, that'd be great! Look at this. These instructions don't make any sense at all, do they? How do the legs fit onto there?

**G** Oh, this flatpack stuff is a real pain. You should have seen me trying to put up my son's new wardrobe. What a joke. You'd have had a good laugh if you'd been there, I can tell you. Anyway, let's have a look.

**M** Here you are.

**G** Hmm. I think there're some bits missing. Look at the diagram here. You need a small piece like that to put these together.

**M** I don't believe it! You mean they haven't given me all the parts? This has gone beyond a joke! I'm going to phone and complain right now. Oh, I wish I'd never bought the stupid thing in the first place. I should have remembered that I'm no good at this sort of thing.

**G** Calm down, Mark. If the worst comes to the worst, they'll just have to give you your money back.

**M** It's just that I'm fed up with the whole thing already. And I've still got to try and fix the computer.

**G** I know. I know. This sort of thing drives me mad, too. Oh, look, what's this at the bottom of the box? Here are your missing parts, if I'm not mistaken!

**M** Oh, what an idiot! I could kick myself! Thanks, Greg. You've saved the day.

I'll buy you a pint in the pub this evening, if you like.

**G** Well, if all goes well from now on, you might just be finished by then!

## Unit 12

**T 12.3**

**N** I want to do something different for our holidays this year. Ideally, something adventurous for a change.

**E** Really? What sort of thing?

**N** Dunno, actually. Maybe going to a lake and learning watersports. Apparently, windsurfing is exciting and we could also learn to sail.

**E** It doesn't sound much fun to me. Personally, I prefer something a bit more relaxing. Basically, I think we work hard enough all year so that we deserve to do nothing somewhere nice for a couple of weeks.

**N** But I'm fed up with lying on a beach and all that. We can do that any old time. It's high time we had some new experiences in life. After all, we don't get much holiday a year.

**E** Well, obviously, I'm very impressed with your new lease of life. However, I'm still not sure what you have in mind or if I want to do it, too.

**N** Let's have a look on the Internet, and see what sort of thing there is. Hopefully, we can find something that suits us both.

**E** Oh, OK then. But I'm not promising anything.

...

**E** Oh, look. Now that's what I call a holiday!

**N** The Maldives? Small beach islands in the middle of the Indian Ocean? Not on your life! Obviously, you weren't paying attention to a thing I was saying! Anyway, they're far too expensive.

**E** No, but look! Look what you can do! There are windsurfing and scuba-diving lessons. Presumably, there'll be sailing lessons, too. Yes, look. Sailing. Even something called paragliding. No idea what that is, though.

**N** Hmm. Sounds interesting, actually. Still, you can bet your life that it'll cost a fortune.

**E** In fact, it's not too bad if you go off-season. Look here at the prices. And off-season a lot of the activities are included in the price. Oh, please let's go. Personally, I've always wanted to go to a desert island. It looks idyllic. It'll be the holiday of a lifetime!

**N** But you don't want an action holiday.

**E** I don't have to have one. I can lie on the beach and watch you exhausting yourself. That's my idea of a good time!

**N** Charming, I must say! Well, let's find out more about it. Get your coat. We're off to the travel agent's. Actually, we'd better go to the bank first. Come on. There's no time to lose.

**E** Wow! OK, then. I'm coming.

**N** And I bet I can get you onto a boat by the end of the holiday!

**E** I told you. I'm not promising anything!

# Answer key

## UNIT 1

**1** 1  2 is walking
3 've been walking
4 was taken
5 'll take
6 had taken
7 have had
8 were having
9 'll be having
10 are … made
11 's been made
12 will have made
13 are being washed
14 had been washed
15 he'd been washing
16 sells
17 will be sold
18 will have been teaching
20 were being taught

2

| Active | Simple | Continuous |
|---|---|---|
| Present | sells | |
| Past | walked | were having |
| Future | will take | will be having |
| Present Perfect | have had | have been walking |
| Past Perfect | had taken | had been washing |
| Future Perfect | will have made | will have been teaching |

| Passive | Simple | Continuous |
|---|---|---|
| Present | is made | are being washed |
| Past | was taken | were being taught |
| Future | will be sold | |
| Present Perfect | has been made | |
| Past Perfect | had been washed | |
| Future Perfect | will have been sold | |

**2** 2 It's **been** really cold …
3 Arsenal **are playing** really well …
4 I've heard **you're going to have** a baby! Congratulations.
5 … when my friend **called**.
6 When I was a little girl, **I always spent** my pocket money on sweets.
7 **I've been going** out with Paulo for two years …
8 … Perhaps **I'll get** him a new shirt.
9 A one-day strike **has been called** by …
10 The teacher said that Megan had been working hard and **deserved** to pass all her exams.

**3** 1 are … doing
2 are … phoning
3 'm staying
4 've … found
5 've been wanting / 've wanted
6 's
7 miss / 've missed / 've been missing
8 'll be / 're going to be
9 've been sending / 've sent
10 've been writing
11 've bought
12 won't leave
13 'll be able
14 've … visited
15 went
16 was
17 dug
18 sat
19 'm … looking forward
20 'll be waiting

**4** 1  1 Our house was built in the 17th century.
2 My flat's being decorated at the moment.
3 Has the coffee machine been fixed yet?
4 While the new kitchen was being built, we ate in restaurants.
5 We arrived at work to find out that our office had been burgled.
6 She won't be recognized in those dark glasses.

2 1 were caught, left / were leaving
2 is … emptied
3 has been missing
4 were driving, were overtaken
5 had been snowing
6 arrive, 'll be picked up

**5** 1  1 has found  2 has invented  3 are called
4 be lifted  5 is designed / has been designed
6 have been built  7 was … shown  8 wasn't
9 doesn't have  10 are needed  11 don't cost
12 will buy  13 is  14 will … take
15 have spoken / have been speaking to
16 have been made  17 will be  18 will reach

2 1 What has Werner Aisslinger designed?
2 Why are they called Loftcubes?
3 Where were they first shown?
4 Where are they needed?
5 How much will they cost?
6 Who (does he hope) will buy them?
7 Who has he spoken to / been speaking to?
8 When will the Loftcubes be ready?

**6** 3 has (A)  4 did (F)  5 have (F)  6 have (A)
7 didn't (A)  8 done (F)  9 does (A)
10 was (A)  11 is (A)  12 doing (F)

**7** 1 **A** have … got
  **B** 'm having
  **B** 've got, to have

2 **A** have … got
  **B** haven't, Have
  **A** 've had, 've got
  **B** to have

3 **A** 've got to / have to
  **B** haven't got / don't have
  **A** had, Have
  **B** 've got

4 **A** having, 've had, haven't had
  **B** haven't got

**8** 1 blood  2 book  3 water  4 green  5 night
6 case  7 bag  8 rain  9 sun  10 road  11 air
12 day  13 hand  14 ice  15 card  16 land
17 sports  18 book

**9** 1  1 a  2 b  3 a  4 a  5 b  6 a

2 1 brought home to me
2 got on like a house on fire
3 make yourselves at home
4 brought the house down
5 as safe as houses
6 hit home

**10** 1  1 out  2 away  3 down  4 off  5 down / in
6 off, on  7 out  8 back  9 in  10 away

2 1 fell out (L)
  fell out (I)
2 put … up (I)
  Put up (L)
3 sorted out (L)
  sort … out (I)
4 stand up (L)
  stand up (I)
5 Hold on (I)
  hold on (L)
6 take … off (L)
  take off (I)
7 picked … up (I)
  pick … up (L)

**11** **1** 1 friend  2 English  3 clean  4 month
5 took  6 group  7 slam  8 box  9 thought
10 work  11 chart  12 winter

**2**

| /e/ | /ɪ/ | /iː/ | /ʌ/ |
|---|---|---|---|
| letter | busy | tree | mother |
| weather | women | heat | fun |
| breakfast | building | machine | worry |
| /ʊ/ | /uː/ | /æ/ | /ɒ/ |
| good | cool | camp | sock |
| woman | suit | family | odd |
| could | shoe | accent | want |
| /ɔː/ | /ɜː/ | /ɑː/ | /ə/ |
| floor | early | father | machine |
| walk | work | garden | father |
| daughter | search | banana | banana |

**12** **1** 1 ✗  2 ✓  3 ✗  4 ✗  5 ✓  6 ✗  7 ✗  8 ✗

**2** 1 drop in
2 That's a drag.
3 a big shot
4 I don't get it.
5 not feel up to something
6 Cheers.

**3** (I) Hope that's OK.
(That's) Absolutely fine.
(It's) Nice to see you.
(I) Haven't seen you for a while, Jerry!
(I've) Just (been) working hard.
(He) Thinks he's such a big shot.
(I) Don't know why.
(Are you going to) Change jobs?
(I) Can't afford it.

## UNIT 2

**1** **1** 1 I've written to Auntie Fay to wish her happy birthday.
I've been writing my essay all morning.
2 I've lost my car keys.
I've been losing weight recently.
3 They've missed the train.
They've been missing you lots, so come home soon.
4 She's been talking on the phone for ages.
She's talked about this subject before.
5 Paula's been leaving work late all this week.
Paula's left work early today to meet her uncle.
6 The cat's been going to our neighbour's to have its dinner.
The cat's gone upstairs.
7 He's had a heart attack.
He's been having second thoughts about accepting the job.
8 I've been saving up to buy a new television.
I've saved up about £200.
9 I've been swimming, which is why my hair is wet.
I've swum twenty lengths today.
10 I've been finding it difficult to concentrate recently.
I've found my cheque book at last.

**2** 2 's been snowing
3 have … travelled
4 have lived; have been trying; haven't managed
5 have been arguing
6 've eaten
7 have been running
8 has been crying; has failed
9 've been sunbathing

**2** *Possible answers:*
1 In Fukushima, Japan.
2 Which school did she go to?
3 How long has she been climbing?
Since she was 10 (years old).
4 What did she study at university?
English and American literature.
5 How long has she been married?
For 38 years.
6 What did she do when she was 30?
She started the first women's climbing club in Japan.
7 When did she climb Mount Everest?
When she was 36.
8 Who gave / awarded her a medal?
The King of Nepal.
9 How many mountains has she climbed?
113.
10 Has she had an exciting life?
Yes, she has.

**3** **1** 1 is standing  2 is actually watching
3 is climbing  4 has been climbing
5 has nearly reached  6 has already climbed
7 started climbing  8 broke  9 became
10 has been named  11 trains  12 has been preparing  13 will climb  14 haven't seen

**2** 2 's (been) taking  3 arrived  4 didn't enjoy
5 're … staying  6 're going  7 's chosen
8 's called  9 will be  10 've done
11 will make  12 won't be  13 'm looking
14 sounds  15 've been training
16 've prepared  17 get  18 'll become

**4** **1** 1 The mail has already been delivered.
2 Have the street lights been repaired yet?
3 Some new anti-smoking laws have just been passed.
4 No new homes have been built for twenty years.
5 The plants haven't been watered.

**2** 2 A yachtsman has been rescued dramatically in the Pacific Ocean.
3 Valuable jewels have been stolen from Sotheby's.
4 A missing boy has been found alive.
5 Euro MPs have been given a huge pay rise.
6 Two hundred and sixty people have been killed in the monsoon in India.
7 An ancient tomb has been discovered in Egypt.
8 Two thousand people have been made redundant in a shock announcement by Ferrari.

**5** **1** 2 have her ears pierced
3 have my eyes tested
4 have had their car serviced
5 had our television repaired yet

**2** Recently …
He's had the invitations printed.
They've had the cake decorated.
Yesterday …
They had the champagne delivered.
He had his hair cut.
Today …
She's having her hair done.
They're having the flowers delivered.
Next week …
They'll have had the photos developed.
She'll have had her wedding dress dry-cleaned.

**6** **1** 1 do  2 make  3 doing  4 do  5 make  6 do
7 do  8 done  9 made  10 made  11 Made
12 does  13 do

**2** 1 made the big time
2 have done without you
3 made off with it
4 make up for
5 could do with
6 make of her
7 make … in time

**7** **1**

|  | car | bus | bike | train | plane | ship/ferry |
|---|---|---|---|---|---|---|
| get into/out of | ✓ | | | | | |
| get on/off | | ✓ | ✓ | ✓ | ✓ | ✓ |
| take off | | | | ✓ | | |
| land | | | | ✓ | | |
| ride | | | ✓ | | | |
| drive | ✓ | ✓ | | ✓ | | |
| catch | | ✓ | | ✓ | ✓ | ✓ |
| miss | | ✓ | | ✓ | ✓ | ✓ |
| board | | ✓ | | ✓ | ✓ | ✓ |
| park | ✓ | ✓ | | | | |

**2** **car:** seat belt, traffic lights, service station, tyres, one-way street, traffic jam, Customs, tunnel, horn
**bus:** traffic lights, seaon ticket, tyres, one-way street, traffic jam, timetable, horn
**bike:** crash helmet, traffic lights, tyres, one-way street, cycle lane
**train:** platform, carriage, ticket collector, season ticket, trolley, track, timetable, Customs, tunnel, porter
**plane:** runway, life jacket, tyres, cargo, check-in desk, timetable, hand luggage, Customs, aisle seat, charter flight
**ship/ferry:** harbour, life jacket, trolley, cargo, port, timetable, Customs, deck, porter, cabin

**8** 1 at  2 out of  3 across / into  4 to  5 through
6 towards  7 off  8 onto  9 over  10 into
11 past / through  12 to  13 into  14 against
15 in  16 out of  17 along  18 past  19 across
20 over  21 up  22 onto

**9** 1  1 explorer; exploration
2 Japan; Japanese
3 contribute; contribution
4 industry; industrial
5 economy; economics
6 politics; politician

2, 3

| •● | •●• | ●•• |
|---|---|---|
| Japan | contribute | industry |
| abroad | develop | politics |
| unique | destruction | backpacker |
| destroy | pollution | calculate |
| unspoilt | illegal | paradise |

| ••● | ••●• | •●•• |
|---|---|---|
| Japanese | contribution | industrial |
| Vietnam | economics | economy |
| | politician | discovery |
| | information | kilometre |
| | European | environment |
| | destination | inhabitant |
| | diarrhoea | |

**10** 1  1 ✗ 2 ✓ 3 ✗ 4 ✓ 5 ✗ 6 ✗ 7 ✓ 8 ✗

2  1 A 2 A 3 M 4 M 5 M 6 M 7 M
8 M 9 S 10 A

3  1 like; and stuff like that
2 sort of; like
3 kind of
4 sort of
5 like
6 and everything

**UNIT 3**

**1** 1,2  1 fell ✗ 2 had fallen ✗ 3 had torn ✗
4 tore ✗ 5 cost ✓ 6 had cost ✓
7 had never flown ✗ 8 flew ✗
9 had caught ✓ 10 caught ✓
11 were ✗ 12 had been ✗

**2** 1 was living; met
2 played; were winning; lost
3 wasn't thinking; had
4 was coughing; didn't get
5 was sunbathing; heard; appeared; landed
6 was snowing; got up; were making;
put; raced
7 was playing; hit; made

**3** 2 was standing  3 heard  4 went back in
5 was  6 said  7 has been  8 managed
9 had been surfing  10 had been knocked
11 had hit  12 swam  13 pulled  14 had just
finished  15 shouted  16 called  17 had to
18 was trying  19 were getting  20 reached
21 had taken  22 felt  23 was recovering
24 wasn't  25 had moved  26 have been

**4** 1  2 a 3 d 4 c 5 b 6 i 7 f 8 g 9 j 10 h 11 m
12 n 13 o 14 l 15 k

2  1 Two years ago, while I was working
in Paris, my grandfather died.
2 As soon as I had fed the cat, I did
my homework.
3 First I had a shower and then I got
dressed.
4 Since I was a child I had always wanted
to visit Australia, and I finally went
last year.
5 As he posted the letter, he realized that
he hadn't put a stamp on it.
6 By the time he'd finshed speaking, most
of the audience had fallen asleep.
7 Once I'd told him the truth I felt better.
8 Until I found a flat I had stayed / been
staying with friends for months.

**5** 2 A Roman temple was discovered
underneath the new housing estate.
3 The races were held indoors because it
was raining.
4 The leisure centre had been booked for a
children's party on Saturday.
5 The dishwasher was being repaired,
so I couldn't leave the house.
6 Our hotel room still hadn't been cleaned
when we returned.
7 The fish hadn't been cooked for long
enough.
8 New traffic lights were being put up at the
crossroads.

**6** 1 was shown
2 liked
3 is regarded
4 felt
5 had been made
6 tells
7 has … been rescued
8 's married
9 is (being) introduced
10 doesn't make
11 is voiced
12 was / is based
13 was not written
14 ends
15 are
16 will … be loved / are … loved

**7**

| Poetry | Prose | Drama |
|---|---|---|
| nursery rhyme | plot | plot |
| critic | chapter | critic |
| review | critic | director |
| character | best-seller | backstage |
| verse | review | script |
| | character | review |
| | novelist | character |
| | blockbuster | leading role |
| | fairytale | verse |
| | setting | setting |
| | whodunnit | rehearsal |
| | science fiction | performance |
| | hardback | playwright |
| | thriller | act |
| | autobiography | full house |
| | paperback | |

**8** 1  2 end a relationship
3 wait a minute
4 talk louder
5 begin a journey
6 not go out, stay at home
7 have a calmer, more stable life
8 arrive
9 be happier
10 be quiet

2  1 turns up  2 set off  3 Cheer up
4 stay in  5 settled down  6 broke up
7 find out  8 Shut up  9 Hold on
10 Speak up

**9** 1  1 pay /peɪ/
2 write /raɪt/
3 phone /fəʊn/
4 round /raʊnd/
5 dear /dɪə/
6 boy /bɔɪ/
7 tour /tʊə/
8 fair /feə/

2  4 /uː/    3 /əʊ/
5 /ɔː/    6 /ɜː/
8 /ɜː/    7 /ɪə/
10 /ɜː/    9 /ɔː/
11 /aʊ/   12 /əʊ/
13 /uː/   14 /əʊ/
17 /uːz/  15 /əʊz/   16 /əʊs/
19 /uːz/  18 /uːs/
22 /ɒm/   21 /uːm/   20 /əʊm/
23 /ɒl/   24 /əʊl/
26 /ʌm/   25 /əʊm/
27 /eɪ/   28 /eɪ/
29 /eɪ/   30 /e/
33 /ʊ/    32 /uː/    31 /ʌ/
35 /ʊd/   34 /əʊld/
38 /əʊ/   36 /ʌ/    37 /ɒ/

**10** 1  1 A programme about a family in
the States.
2 The mother was sent to a secret home
for unmarried mothers, and the baby
was taken away from her.
3 In Vietnam; he was a soldier.
4 The girl and the baby's father.
5 That she had a brother.
6 San Francisco.
7 Some new friends.
8 Her brother.
9 She was over the moon.
10 That they had both moved to San
Francisco, chosen the same area to
live in, and made the same friends.

2 a 8  b 6  c 1  d 4  e 2  f 3  g 5
h 10  i 7  j 9

## UNIT 4

**1** 1 don't   2 didn't   3 haven't   4 aren't
5 isn't   6 won't   7 'm not   8 doesn't
9 hadn't   10 hasn't

**2** 5 not   6 n't   7 not   8 not   9 no   10 Not
11 none   12 no   13 n't   14 not   15 Not
16 none   17 No   18 no   19 None   20 Not

**3** 2 I told you not to go to work. Why aren't you in bed?
3 Tom was an unsuccessful businessman who didn't achieve much in his life.
4 Our house is easy/isn't difficult to find. No one ever gets lost.
5 We had a terrible time in Venice. There were so many people there.
6 You mustn't exercise/must rest your ankle. Try not to move it at all. / Try to move it as little as possible.
7 I needn't/don't have to iron my shirt. I'm not going out/I'm staying in tonight.
8 You don't have to come with me. I'll go on my own.
9 I wasn't in a hurry, because I didn't have to/need to go to the shops.
10 None of the students passed the exam, so their teacher was angry/disappointed.

**4** 2 I don't suppose you've got change for a 20-euro note?
3 This machine doesn't seem to be working.
4 I didn't think it was going to rain.
5 They don't want their daughter to move to Canada.
6 I didn't expect to see you here.
7 I don't suppose you've seen Robert recently?
8 I don't think I'd like snails.
9 I don't expect you remember me.
10 I don't believe she passed all her exams.

**5** 2 Who made the film *Catch Me If You Can*?
3 How old was Frank when he ran away to New York?
4 Why did he run away to New York?
5 What did he look like?
6 What was Frank's first con trick?
7 How much had he collected when the bank found out?
8 How long was Frank a Pan Am pilot?
9 Who did he tell his secret to? / Who called the police?
10 What did he become next/after he was a pilot?
11 What did Frank teach at university?
12 When was he eventually arrested?
13 How long did he spend in prison?
14 What has he been doing since then?

**6** 1  1 I'm not sure where he learned how to forge bank cheques.
2 I don't know how he had the nerve to pretend to be a pilot.
3 I'd like to know which countries he visited as a pilot.
4 I've no idea why his girlfriend called the police.
5 I haven't a clue how he managed to pass the bar exam.
6 I can't imagine who gave him a job as a doctor.

7 I wonder why the police took so long to catch him.
8 Do you know what he thought of prison?

2  1 I wish I knew why he told his secret to his girlfriend.
2 Have you any idea how many attempts it took him to pass the bar exam?
3 Why do you think he went to France?
4 Can you tell me how long he spent in prison?
5 Do you know what he is doing now/ what has happened to him since then?

**7** 1  2 by   3 to   4 at   5 on   6 in   7 about
8 of   9 from   10 with

2  2 What for?   3 Where to?   4 What about?   5 How long for?   6 Who for?
7 Who to?   8 What with?

**8** 1 b   2 a   3 c   4 d   5 e   6 f   7 h   8 g   9 i
10 j   11 l   12 k

**9** *Sample answers:*
1 was it like
2 Who did you talk to
3 How is she
4 How come
5 can't you
6 is it
7 Who's he
8 What does he look like
9 Didn't he/Did he
10 Why/How come
11 Who
12 What's … going to do

**10** 1, 2

| Adjectives | |
|---|---|
| unreal | fake |
| incredible | unbelievable |
| implausible | ridiculous |
| improbable | unlikely |
| displeased | annoyed |
| abnormal | bizarre |
| unprofessional | amateur |
| unimportant | trivial |
| **Nouns** | |
| dishonesty | deceit |
| unreality | fantasy |
| disbelief | incredulity |
| **Verbs** | |
| disappear | vanish |
| misunderstand | confuse |
| mistrust/distrust | suspect |
| uncover | reveal |

**11** 1  **keep:** a promise, in touch with sb, going, a secret, sb waiting, fit
**lose:** your way, your temper

2  1 keep in touch   2 lost … temper
3 keep a secret   4 keep … waiting;
lost … way   5 Keep calm
6 keep fit; lose weight

**12** 2 for   3 at   4 of/from   5 from   6 in
7 to   8 in   9 in   10 to/with   11 to,
about   12 at   13 in, with   14 for   15 in

**13** 1  2 wasn't it (fall)   3 could you (rise)
4 isn't he (fall)   5 isn't it (fall)
6 aren't I (fall)   7 have you (rise)
8 weren't we (fall)   9 would you (rise)

2  2 That was a really tasteless meal, wasn't it? (fall)
3 You've borrowed my new coat again, haven't you? ( fall)
4 You couldn't/wouldn't water my plants, could/would you? (rise)
5 Vanessa, you're going on a business trip to Rome, aren't you? (rise)

## UNIT 5

**1** 1 You're going to work harder from now on, aren't you?
2 I'll see you next week, won't I?
3 Kate's leaving soon, isn't she?
4 You'll ring when you get there, won't you?
5 Our plane takes off at 4 p.m., doesn't it?
6 The decorators will have finished by next week, won't they?
7 You aren't getting married next week, are you?
8 We won't need tickets to get in, will we?
9 We'll be millionaires one day, won't we?
10 Max won't be coming, will he?

**2** 1 'm going to, 'll
2 are going to, 'll
3 'm going to, 'll, 'll
4 will, 'll
5 'm … going to, 'll
6 'll, going to, 'll
7 'm going to, 'll
8 'll, 'll

**3** 2 I'll buy her a present.
3 I'm going to study hard for my exams.
4 I'm seeing/going to see the dentist next Friday.
5 I think Manchester United will win on Saturday.
6 I'm sorry. I'm going to be late for the meeting.
7 My sister is expecting / having a baby in March.
8 My plane leaves at 7.30 a.m.
9 This time next week I'll be lying on a beach in Spain.
10 I think it'll be hot there.

**4** 3 I'll be living in New York.
4 I'll have paid off my student bank loan.
5 I'll be earning at least $100,000 a year.
6 I'll be eating out at least four times a week.
7 I'll be running in Central Park every day.
8 I'll have got/be getting very fit.
9 I'll have married an American.
10 I'll have had two children.

**5** 1 're going to celebrate
2 'll be buying
3 'll never leave
4 won't happen
5 'll be married
6 will you be doing
7 'm going to record
8 will you be looking for

9 'm going to change
10 'm going to do
11 've been getting
12 'll have made up
13 'll have
14 'll be concentrating
15 'll be able to

6  2 A What are you doing   B ✓
   3 A ✓   B What shall I do?
   4 A is getting married   B ✓
   5 A ✓   B You'll have to wake me up.
   6 A ✓   B You'll be getting
   7 A ✓   B It'll only take
   8 A ✓   B We're going to stay at home.
   9 A as soon as I arrive   B ✓

7  1 eat, won't get
   2 won't move, 've found
   3 'll love, meet
   4 Will you / Are you going to learn, are
   5 won't go, have/have had
   6 'll be, finish/'ve finished
   7 don't do, will you have to
   8 are, will deal
   9 will feel, 've had
   10 've tried, 'll never use

8  1 Put   2 taking   3 Put   4 take   5 putting
   6 take   7 putting   8 taken   9 take
   10 take   11 takes   12 take   13 take
   14 put   15 put

9  1 a 're waiting for
     b is expected
     c looking forward to
   2 a spend/'ve been spending/spent
     b pass
     c wasted
   3 a Have … seen
     b watched/were watching
     c Look at
   4 a Actually
     b at the moment
     c really
   5 a owe
     b borrowed
     c lend
   6 a embarrassed
     b nervous
     c angry

10 3 I couldn't take them all in.
   4 I'll sort it out tomorrow.
   5 Put it in your diary.
   6 Please put them away.
   7 … you'd better look after him.
   8 I'll look into it right away.
   9 Take it back!
   10 … you've put me off her.

11 1 1 won't /əʊ/   2 walk /ɔː/   3 wonder /ʌ/
     4 woman /ʊ/   5 warm /ɔː/   6 word /ɜː/
     7 wear /eə/   8 weight /eɪ/   9 want /ɒ/
     10 work /ɜː/   11 wander /ɒ/
     12 women /ɪ/   13 worm /ɜː/
     14 ward /ɔː/   15 weary /ɪə/
     16 weird /ɪə/

2  1 phone /əʊ/   2 blood /ʌ/   3 love /ʌ/
   4 through /uː/   5 weak /iː/   6 lower /əʊ/
   7 north /ɔː/   8 height /aɪ/   9 pear /eə/
   10 hear /ɪə/

1  1 luggage   2 food   3 cash
   4 unemployment   5 music   6 violence
   7 traffic   8 opportunity   9 ingredient
   10 fluid

2  1 any   2 some, any   3 Some, any
   4 some, any   5 any, any   6 some, some

3  2 Is there much work to be done in the
     garden?
   3 I didn't spend much time on the
     homework.
   4 Did they do much research before they
     found a cure?
   5 They could't give me much information
     about the delay in our flight.
   6 I didn't have too many problems with
     this exercise.
   7 I've got too much luggage. I can't carry
     it all.
   8 There is too much traffic on the streets I
     of our town.

4  1 *Sample answers:*
     1 There are lots of cheese sandwiches.
     2 There are a few ham sandwiches.
     3 There's a huge amount of spaghetti.
     4 There's only a little rice and
       vegetable curry.
     5 There are several hamburgers.
     6 There are no chips.
     7 There isn't much fruit salad.
     8 There are a couple of bananas.
     9 There aren't many doughnuts.
     10 There's hardly any apple juice.

2  3 's lots / a huge amount   4 a few
   5 's only a little   6 aren't any / are none (left)
   7 a little   8 are a few   9 's only a little (left)
   10 've got a couple   11 a little   12 lots

5  2 a few   3 have less respect … than
   4 few   5 a little   6 Fewer   7 Few   8 a few
   9 is little …   10 a few

6  1 1 somewhere   2 anyone/anybody
     3 anywhere   4 anything   5 everything
     6 nothing   7 Nobody/No one
     8 nowhere   9 someone/somebody
     10 something, anything   11 anyone/
     anybody   12 Everyone/Everybody

2  1 b   2 a   3 c   4 d   5 f   6 e   7 h   8 g
   9 i   10 j   11 l   12 k   13 m   14 n   15 o
   16 p

7  1 1 much   2 nobody   3 A couple   4 little
     5 few   6 multi   7 all   8 any   9 hardly any
     10 enough   11 a bit   12 part   13 more
     14 piece   15 None   16 any   17 more than
     18 no   19 something   20 several
     21 over   22 a lot   23 all   24 a great deal of
     25 some

2  2 600 shillings is very little/not very much
     money.
   3 Odonga has a lot of friends.
   4 None of the young people in his village
     have jobs.
   5 It took him several hours to write
     the letter.
   6 There were no jobs available at the
     company.
   7 Conrad Millbank heard about his story.
   8 Until now, Odonga hasn't had much
     good fortune in his life.

8  1 a piece of cake/paper/bread
     a jar of honey
     a slice of bread/cake
     a tube of toothpaste
     a piece of cake/paper/bread
     a loaf of bread
     a bar of soap/chocolate
     a box of chocolates
     a tin of soup
     a can of beer/soup/cola
     a bottle of beer/cola
     a sheet of paper

2  1 a piece/slice of cake
   2 a tin/can of soup
   3 sheets of paper
   4 a box of chocolates
   5 bar of chocolate
   6 slice of bread
   7 many cans/bottles of beer
   8 bar of soap
   9 a jar of special honey

9  1 A **on** foot
     **under** arrest
     **over/under** £500
     **above/below/over/under** 75%
     **above/below** freezing
     **over/under** 18 years old
     **under** new management
     **on** holiday
     **under** pressure
     **on** business

   B **during/in** the night
     **by/on** New Year's Day
     **by/during/in** the winter
     **by/on** Friday afternoon
     **at/by** the weekend
     **in/on** time
     **in** a fortnight's time
     **during/in** the rush hour
     **in** his forties

2  1 in   2 under   3 Over   4 over   5 Over
   6 above   7 on   8 at   9 over   10 During
   11 on   12 under   13 under   14 in
   15 in

10 1 Ellen Miles is calling John Barker about
     an order she made which hasn't arrived.

2  1 ✓   2 ✗   3 ✗   4 ✗   5 ✗   6 ✓

3  1 R   2 J   3 J   4 E   5 J   6 J   7 E   8 E

**4** 1 How can I help you?
  2 I'm putting you through now.
  3 an order I placed with you
  4 a week maximum
  5 Do you have the order code to hand?
  6 that all seems to be in order
  7 I'll get back to you before 12.

**11** 1 1 V  2 N  3 V  4 N  5 N  6 V
       7 N  8 V  9 N  10 V  11 V  12 N

## UNIT 7

**1** 2 b  3 b  4 a  5 b  6 b  7 a  8 b

**2** 1 1 should/ought to/must
       2 Can/May/Could
       3 must/have to
       4 can
       5 may/might/will/could
       6 can/could
       7 have to
       8 must/should/ought to/may/might
       9 can/could/ought to/must/should
      10 have to/must

   2 1 won't
       2 don't have to
       3 couldn't
       4 won't
       5 can't
       6 was able to
       7 mustn't

**3** 1 You mustn't stop here.
  2 We don't have to learn the whole poem.
  3 They didn't have to take off their shoes.
  4 He can't be speaking Swedish.
  5 We didn't have to wear a uniform at school.
  6 You won't have to/need to help me do this exercise.

**4** 1 1 has to have  2 won't  3 said she'd
       4 couldn't  5 she had  6 should
       7 you must  8 she might  9 can  10 will
      11 can't  12 have to  13 can only
      14 'll  15 ought to  16 You may/ might
      17 You mustn't  18 couldn't
      19 You should/might/could
      20 You must / have to

   2 1 … I'd better buy her a card.
       2 Guests are advised not to leave …
       3 Smoking is only permitted …
       4 He's bound to pass …
       5 The use of dictionaries is not allowed in this exam.
       6 People under 18 aren't supposed to drink alcohol.
       7 Travellers to the States are required to have a visa.
       8 You are likely to find/It is likely that you'll find …
       9 … I promised to help Jane.
      10 My parents didn't let me …

**5** 1 2 She must be missing her boyfriend.
       3 It'll be Tom.
       4 She can't still be sleeping.
       5 They could be having a party.
       6 He must have a deadline to meet.
       7 It might be difficult to drive to work.
       8 She may be hiding in the garden.

**2** 1 should go
    2 might feel
    3 must finish
    4 'll pass
    5 should be touching down
    6 must be
    7 can't be
    8 could be snowing
    9 can snow
   10 must be making
   11 might be
   12 could be

**6** 1 1 V  2 M  3 V  4 V  5 M  6 V
       7 V  8 M

   2 1 needn't/don't have to
       2 mustn't
       3 needn't/don't have to
       4 need to/have to
       5 don't have to
       6 got to
       7 needs

**7** 1 His debts will take ages to pay off.
       He accumulated debts of £2,000.
       Inflation went up by 2%.
       She contributes to the household bills.
       I earned £2,000 in interest.
       My credit card expires at the end of July.
       I changed some traveller's cheques.
       The exchange rate is good just now.

   2 1 check-out  2 added  3 bill  4 pay
       5 salary  6 by cheque  7 overdrawn
       8 credit card  9 cash  10 reduce
      11 came to  12 saving  13 change
      14 receipt

**8** 2 off with  3 down on  4 on with  5 up for
   6 away with  7 out of  8 out with, off with
   9 up with  10 on with, out with

**9** 1 1 c  2 b  3 b  4 c  5 c  6 b

   2 1 a bit upset
       2 one or two hurtful
       3 a bit of trouble at work
       4 down a bit
       5 hasn't been great

**10** 1 doesn't
    2 shouldn't
    3 mustn't
    4 promised
    5 strapped
    6 distinctly
    7 special
    8 arranged
    9 relationship
   10 comfortable
   11 excitement
   12 impressed

**11** 1 **Alan** Don't you think Frank's put on a lot of weight recently?
       **Kevin** You're <u>kid</u>ding. If <u>anything</u>, he's <u>lost</u> weight.

   2 **Alan** I think Frank earns more than me.
       **Kevin** Well, I know he earns a <u>lot</u> more than <u>me</u>.

3 **Alan** He's thinking of buying a second-hand Mercedes.
  **Kevin** What do you mean? He's already bought a <u>brand new</u> one.

4 **Alan** He's just bought two pairs of designer jeans.
  **Kevin** Didn't you <u>know</u> that <u>all</u> Frank's clothes are designer labels?

5 **Alan** Does Frank have many stocks and shares?
  **Kevin** He has <u>loads</u> of them.

6 **Alan** Isn't Frank in New York on business?
  **Kevin** <u>No</u>, in <u>fact</u> he's in <u>Florida</u> on <u>holiday</u>.

7 **Alan** His latest girlfriend has long, blonde hair.
  **Kevin** <u>Really</u>? The girl <u>I</u> saw him with had <u>short, brown</u> hair.

## UNIT 8

**1** 1 b  2 c  3 a  4 b  5 b  6 a  7 b  8 c

**2** 1 1 D  2 D  3 ND  4 D  5 ND  6 D
       7 ND  8 D  9 ND  10 ND

   2 1 I'd love to meet someone who could teach me how to cook.
       2 We're looking for a house which has four bedrooms.
       3 We went to see *Romeo and Juliet*, which I really enjoyed.
       4 Do you know a shop that sells second-hand furniture?
       5 Marilyn Monroe, whose real name was Norma Jean Baker, died of a drug overdose.
       6 I find people who lose their temper difficult to get on with.
       7 My computer, which I bought just last year, is already out of date.
       8 I met a girl I went to school with.
       9 Professor James Williams, who many people consider to be the world's expert on volcanoes, will give a talk next week.
      10 I bought a ham and pickle sandwich, which I ate immediately.

**3** 4 The thing I most regret is not going to university.
   5 My two daughters, who are 16 and 13, are both interested in dancing.
   6 no change
   7 no change
   8 no change
   9 Salt, whose qualities have been known since prehistoric times, is used to season and preserve food.
  10 The CD I bought yesterday doesn't work.
  11 no change
  12 The Algarve, where my mother's family comes from, is famous for its beautiful beaches and dramatic coastline.

**4** 1 1 how much I love you?
　　2 what I believe to be right.
　　3 which was a nightmare.
　　4 where my brother lives.
　　5 whose hair came down to her waist.
　　6 which came as a bit of a surprise.
　　7 when you expect to arrive.
　　8 whatever you want.

　2 1 who　2 that/which　3 where　4 which
　　5 —　6 whose　7 which　8 —　9 —
　　10 that　11 whose　12 —　13 where
　　14 which　15 Whatever

**5** 2 She's a friend (who) I can always rely on.
　　3 That's the man (who) the police were looking for.
　　4 She recommended a book by Robert Palmer, who I'd never heard of.
　　5 The suit (that) I paid £400 for has been reduced to to £200.
　　6 This is the book (that) I was telling you about.
　　7 The Prime Minister, whose views I agree with, gave a good speech.
　　8 He spoke about the environment, which I care deeply about.
　　9 What's that music you're listening to?
　　10 My mother, who I looked after for many years, died last week.

**6** 3 screaming　4 satisfied　5 disgusting
　　6 confusing　7 exposed　8 conceited
　　9 frightening　10 exhausting
　　11 disappointing　12 tiring　13 unexpected
　　14 disturbing　15 thrilling　16 relaxing
　　17 disappointed　18 well-behaved
　　19 promising　20 loaded

**7** 1 2 People living in blocks of flats …
　　3 Letters posted before …
　　4 The train standing on …
　　5 Firemen have rescued passengers trapped …
　　6 … house overlooking the River Thames.
　　7 … litter dropped by the crowds.

　2 2 finishing　3 stolen　4 saying
　　5 Feeling　6 borrowed　7 knowing
　　8 explaining　9 Taking　10 studying

**8** 1 j　2 b　3 d　4 g　5 c　6 m　7 l　8 n
　　9 a　10 e　11 i　12 k　13 f　14 h

**9** 1 **People:** stubborn, thrilled, spoilt, aggressive, exhausted, easy-going
　　**Places:** breathtaking, picturesque, deserted, desolate, overcrowded
　　**Things:** automatic, hand-made, accurate, waterproof, long-lasting, priceless

　2 1 breathtaking　2 long-lasting
　　3 automatic　4 easy-going　5 unspoilt
　　6 picturesque 7 stubborn, spoilt
　　8 hand-made　9 overcrowded, deserted

**10** 1 a ten-pound note
　　2 a four-week language course
　　3 a three-hour drive
　　4 a three-course meal
　　5 a two-week holiday
　　6 a two-hour delay
　　7 a ten-page letter

　　8 a three-year university course
　　9 a ten-year prison sentence
　　10 a five-star hotel
　　11 a 30 mph-speed limit
　　12 a two hundred-year-old house

**11** 1 of　2 with, for　3 for　4 of　5 of　6 in
　　7 from, to　8 about　9 to　10 of　11 of
　　12 for　13 for　14 with　15 about

**12** 1 **A:** executive, inhabitant, distinctly, rebuilt, eccentric, insect, lamp, sumptuous, anonymous, citizen, documentary, landscape, temperature, business
　　**B:** receipt, fasten, exhausted, whistle, straight, fascinating, delighted, debt

　2 1 scientific　2 psychologist　3 handsome
　　4 receipt　5 Christmas　6 nightmare
　　7 climb　8 grandfather　9 Wednesday
　　10 calm

## UNIT 9

**1** 1 1 d　2 g　3 f　4 e　5 h　6 c　7 b　8 i
　　9 j　10 a

　2 Sample answers
　　2 He will insist that he's right about everything.
　　3 She eats it every day after dinner.
　　4 He never stops complaining when the football's on TV.
　　5 They're always bringing home new things for the house.
　　6 He can't talk about anything else.
　　7 She'll watch it all day if she gets the chance.
　　8 He never gets angry with anyone.
　　9 They ('ll) never say please or thankyou.
　　10 He's always asking if there's anything he can do to help.

**2** 1 1 used to
　　2 Did you use to
　　3 never used to/didn't use to
　　4 Did you use to
　　5 used to
　　6 didn't use to
　　7 did you use to
　　8 Did you use to

　2 2 a, b, c　3 a　4 a, b, c　5 a, b, c　6 a
　　7 a, b, c　8 a, b　9 a　10 a, b, c

**3** 1 sentences 2, 4, 5, 8, 9

　2 *Sample answers:*
　　1 My dad will mend/will insist on mending his motorbike in the living room.
　　2 My brother never puts the top on the toothpaste.
　　3 My sister's always borrowing my clothes without asking.
　　4 Uncle Tom will smoke cigars in the kitchen.
　　5 My grandpa was always eating toast in bed.
　　6 My grandma would never turn on her hearing aid.

**4** 1 1 aren't used to
　　2 get used to
　　3 'm used to, get used to
　　4 got used to
　　5 used to
　　6 didn't use to
　　7 's used to
　　8 get used to
　　9 Did … use to
　　10 Have … got used to

　2 1 get upset
　　2 'm getting better
　　3 to be a pilot
　　4 'll be ready, 'm … getting dressed, 've been ready
　　5 're lost
　　6 are getting divorced
　　7 get/got to know, / got to like
　　8 'm getting tired
　　9 gets dark

**5** 1 1 b　2 b　3 a　4 a　5 a　6 a　7 a　8 a
　　9 b　10 a　11 b　12 b　13 b　14 b　15 a
　　16 a　17 a　18 a　19 a　20 b　21 b　22 b
　　23 b　24 b　25 b　26 b　27 a　28 b

　2 1 used　2 would　3 used　4 got　5 got
　　6 wasn't　7 got　8 would　9 been

**6** 2 wave　3 point　4 right　5 suit　6 fair
　　7 sort　8 fan　9 train

**7** 1 a bored　　　b board
　　2 a allowed　　b aloud
　　3 a whale　　　b wail
　　4 a caught　　 b court
　　5 a loan　　　 b lone
　　6 a hire　　　 b higher

**8** 1 1 f　2 i　3 l　4 b　5 h　6 g　7 c　8 e
　　9 d　10 a　11 j　12 k

　2 1 broke into
　　2 looked up to
　　3 take … back
　　4 pointed … out
　　5 come up with
　　6 told … off
　　7 deal with
　　8 fit in with
　　9 drop out of
　　10 count on
　　11 brought … up
　　12 broke off

**9** 1 1 c　2 b

　2 1, 3, 5, 6, 8, 9

**10** 1 1 I don't want to see him but I'm sure you want to.
　　2 She isn't going to learn from this experience, but he is.
　　3 I've heard that you're thinking of moving from London. Are you?
　　4 They have dinner at seven, don't they?
　　5 You'll be able to get a ticket for me, won't you?
　　6 I've got no idea who this letter's from.
　　7 Can't you remember who Bill used to work for?
　　8 I've been waiting for you to come. Where were you?

9 We'd been looking forward to coming for ages, then at the last minute we weren't able to.
10 Won't you sit down for a couple of minutes?

2 A What are you doing at the weekend?
B I haven't decided yet.
A We're going to Scotland. Do you want to come too?
B I'd love to. Where are you staying?
A We've decided to camp. None of us can afford to pay for a hotel.
B Camping in Scotland in October! You'll be freezing cold.
A No, we won't, we've got strong tents, lots of warm clothes, and thick sleeping bags.
B Have you checked the weather forecast?
A Of course we have, and it's pretty warm for October.
B OK then. It'll be quite an adventure!
A Excellent! I'll tell the others – they'll be delighted. We'll pick you up at six on Friday. See you then. Goodbye!
B Bye!

<h2>UNIT 10</h2>

1 2 I had to take the pills three times a day.
3 They must have been away on holiday.
4 We couldn't see the top of the mountain.
5 He can't have been be a millionaire.
6 We weren't allowed to shout in the classroom.
7 He wouldn't go to bed.
8 That will have been John on the phone.
9 You should have been more careful.
10 You could have helped with the washing-up for a change.

2 1 3 ✓✓ 4 ✓ 5 ✓ 6 ✓✓ 7 ✓✓ 8 ✓✓
9 ✓✓ 10 ✓ 11 ✓ 12 ✓✓

2 *Possible answers:*
If I go to India, I can/will/may/might see the Taj Mahal.
If I went to India, I might/would/could see the Taj Mahal.
If I'd gone to India, I might/would/could have seen the Taj Mahal.

3 1 1 She must have got engaged to Andy.
2 He can't have cut it for ages.
3 They must have been doing something naughty.
4 She must have been making a cake.
5 They might have gone without me.
6 He can't have had a party last night.
7 They must have arrived home by now.
8 She might/must have mislaid my number.

2 1 It must have been blown down by the wind.
2 They must have been washed with something red.
3 It can't have been repaired properly.
4 It can't have been dry-cleaned recently.
5 They can't have been watered while we were away.
6 It must have been hit by a stone.

4 1 could have used
2 might have climbed up
3 needn't have bothered
4 must have been joking
5 can't have spent
6 might have misheard
7 should have phoned
8 may have been delayed
9 needn't have worried
10 shouldn't have burned
11 must have fallen
12 can't have put on

5 1 shouldn't have
2 may have, 'll have
3 'd have, could have, might have, 'd have, needn't have, should have
4 must have

6 1 1 b  2 a  3 b

2 1 would have been
2 must have been lying
3 couldn't have survived
4 may have had
5 must have fallen
6 could hear
7 will have got
8 could have broken
9 must have been talking
10 needn't have been
11 might have died
12 must have been
13 should have done
14 could have been

7 1 heart-to-heart
2 hands full
3 face the fact
4 heart
5 head for business
6 sharp tongue
7 heart of gold
8 put a brave face
9 pulling my leg
10 give her a hand

8 1 

| Physical appearance | Personality |
| --- | --- |
| graceful | moody |
| wrinkled | big-headed |
| skinny | brainy |
| bald | quick-thinking |
| well-buit | nosy |
| smart | cheeky |
| curly | narrow-minded |
|  | affectionate |
|  | smart |
|  | hard-hearted |

2 1 handed  2 elbow  3 thumbed  4 eyed
5 was footing  6 headed  7 are armed
8 shoulder

9 1 2 remind ... of
3 congratulated ... on
4 models ... on
5 hide ... from
6 held ... to
7 invited ... to
8 trick ... into
9 inherit ... from
10 shouted ... at
11 forgive ... for
12 was accused ... of

10 1 

| should | good | food | nude |
| --- | --- | --- | --- |
| bread | said | leaf | chief |
| choose | lose | taught | court |
| toes | knows | chef | deaf |
| hate | weight | through | knew |
| tight | height | wore | pour |
| full | wool | brain | reign |
| pool | fool | leave | grieve |
| blood | mud | foot | put |

2 **The pelican**
A rare old bird is a pelican
His beak can hold more than his belly can
He can take in his beak
Enough food for a week
And I'm damned if I know how the hell he can!

**The lady from Twickenham**
There was a young lady from Twickenham
Whose shoes were too tight to walk quick in them
She came back from a walk
Looking whiter than chalk
And she took them both off and was sick in them!

<h2>UNIT 11</h2>

1 1 1, 4, 8 refer to real past time. The others refer to the hypothetical past.

2 1 ✗  2 ✓  3 ✗  4 ✗  5 ✓  6 ✗  7 ✗  8 ✓

3 2 don't  3 didn't  4 can't  5 is  6 won't
7 do  8 was/have  9 don't/haven't

2 1 I wish you were rich.
I wish you could/would/had come.
I wish I were rich.
I wish I could/had come.

2 1 could, was able to
2 wasn't
3 had
4 hadn't gone
5 have stayed
6 didn't speak, wouldn't speak
7 'd had
8 lived

3 1 1 I wish I'd invited him to the party.
2 You should have been watching the road.
3 If only I hadn't said that to her.
4 I wish I hadn't hit him.
5 I'd rather you didn't tell her.
6 I wish Meg wouldn't stay out so late.
7 I should have worked harder for my exams.

**2** *Sample answers:*
1 I wish I had a Rolls Royce.
2 If only I could get a job/had somwhere to live.
3 If only I could get to sleep. I wish it were/was morning.
4 We should have booked some rooms.
5 I wish I'd bought some petrol.
6 Cat: 'I wish she'd stop playing!'

**4** 1 wish  2 only  3 could  4 would  5 have
6 should  7 hadn't  8 wouldn't  9 unless
10 could  11 would  12 had  13 imagine
14 have  15 had  16 could  17 's
18 realized  19 if  20 hadn't

**5** 1  1 used to work
2 It was boring
3 we were having
4 was coming round
5 could see the face
6 came to a sudden stop
7 I could do
8 would have ended up
9 didn't ever talk
10 was annoyed

2  2 wouldn't have met, hadn't been working
3 couldn't have gone, hadn't picked her up
4 hadn't been talking, wouldn't have crossed
5 hadn't been, wouldn't have crashed
6 wouldn't have blushed, hadn't been
7 hadn't been going, wouldn't have been wearing
8 might have continued, hadn't crashed

3  1 I wouldn't have been ill if I hadn't had the shellfish.
2 I would have phoned you if I had had the time.
3 If I had known the jumper wasn't washable, I wouldn't have bought it.
4 I wouldn't have believed it if I hadn't seen it with my own eyes.

4  2 If I'd known your address, I could/would have sent you a postcard.
3 If I'd remembered when your birthday was, I would have bought you a present.
4 If I hadn't forgotten to set my alarm clock, I wouldn't have been late.
5 If I hadn't been taking my wife to the hospital, I wouldn't have broken the speed limit.

**6** 1 feel, won't go
2 sold, 'd make
3 see, 'll tell
4 hadn't gone, wouldn't have met
5 didn't love, wouldn't be going to marry/wouldn't have married
6 buy, get
7 would … do, saw, would run
8 had brought, would know
9 hadn't had, would have burned down
10 were, 'd apologize
11 eats, gets
12 listened, would have heard, wouldn't be

**7** 1  1 Imagine  2 in case  3 unless  4 Unless
5 Suppose  6 in case  7 Had  8 Should

2  1 I won't come unless they invite me.
2 Supposing he left you?
3 Suppose you had learned to play tennis, would you have been a champion by now?
4 We're going to install a smoke alarm in case there's a fire.
5 She won't get that job unless she learns to speak French.
6 Imagine the lifeguard hadn't been there; what would have happened?
7 I won't go out this evening in case Paul rings.
8 I'll be at my desk until 6.00, should you need to speak to me about the matter.

**8** 1 illegible  2 unreadable  3 childish
4 childlike  5 sensitive  6 sensible
7 truthful  8 true  9 intolerant
10 intolerable  11 economic  12 economical

**9** 1 breakdown  2 comeback  3 check-up
4 outcome  5 outlook  6 outbreak
7 breakthough  8 feedback  9 takeaway
10 downfall

**10** 1  1 Set up a home office.
2 computer, computer table
3 Some of the pieces are missing.
4 He's no good at that sort of thing.
5 Greg; he finds the missing parts.

2  1 b  2 c  3 a  4 e  5 d

3  1 M  2 G  3 G  4 M  5 M  6 M  7 G
8 M

**11** 2 /e/ bread: breath, breadth, thread, deaf, death, health, jealous, lead, leapt, meant, weapon

/i:/ meat: scream, breathe, cheat, beast, heal, lead, leap, reason

/ɪə/ ear: dear, tear, hear, clear, beard, gear, theatre, weary

/eə/ wear: tear, bear, pear, swear

/eɪ/ break: steak, great

/ɜ:/ learn: earth, pearl, search

## UNIT 12

**1** 1  1 a  2 the  3 the  4 a  5 – , a, the
6 the  7 a, –  8 the, –  9 a, The, – , the

2  1 A  2 the  3 a  4 –  5 the  6 a  7 a
8 the  9 a  10 the  11 –  12 the
13 her  14 the  15 a  16 –  17 –  18 –
19 a  20 the  21 The  22 an  23 the
24 the  25 the

**2** 1  1 everything  2 Everything  3 All
4 Every  5 All  6 All  7 everything
8 all  9 Every  10 everybody

2  1 All, none  2 either, both  3 both, neither  4 every  5 no, every  6 every
7 Each  8 either, both  9 Neither
10 Either  11 both, either  12 Each

**3** 1 These  2 This  3 That  4 those  5 that
6 that  7 this  8 these  9 this  10 this
11 that  12 this  13 That  14 those  15 that

**4** 2 the  3 one  4 her  5 a  6 every
7 a great deal of  8 a great deal  9 an
10 enough  11 her  12 a lot of  13 the
14 her  15 all  16 everything  17 those
18 no  19 their  20 most  21 her  22 a
23 several  24 this  25 the  26 her  27 The

**5** 1 back of the chair  2 cat's milk  3 toilet paper  4 parents' advice  5 bottle of wine
6 road sign  7 wine bottles  8 Prime Minister's duties  9 heel of my shoe
10 hairbrush  11 end of the film
12 today's news  13 Underground station
14 parents' wedding anniversary
15 company's success/success of the company
16 fortnight's holiday  17 government's economic policy  18 rate of inflation
19 coffee cups  20 cup of coffee

**6** 1 **be:** on the safe side, in touch with sb, no point in doing sth, on one's mind, up to date
**have:** the nerve to do sth, a word with sb, no chance of doing sth

2  2 have the right to
3 will be in touch with
4 is … on my mind
5 have a word with
6 had the nerve to
7 to be on the safe side
8 have no chance of
9 no point in
10 have been in touch with

**7** 1 out of  2 in  3 on, by  4 for  5 in
6 between  7 for  8 to  9 about  10 with
11 to  12 of  13 before/by  14 in  15 to

**8** 1  1 T  2 F  3 F  4 F  5 T  6 T

2  1 Apparently  2 Personally  3 After all
4 Hopefully  5 Obviously  6 Presumably
7 Still  8 In fact

**9**
| Noun | | Verb | |
|---|---|---|---|
| advice | /əd'vaɪs/ | to ad'vise | /əd'vaɪz/ |
| use | /ju:s/ | to use | /ju:z/ |
| abuse | /əb'ju:s/ | to abuse | /əb'ju:z/ |
| belief | /bɪ'li:f/ | to believe | /bɪ'li:v/ |
| relief | /rɪ'li:f/ | to relieve | /rɪ'li:v/ |
| grief | /gri:f/ | to grieve | /gri:v/ |
| excuse | /ɪks'kju:s/ | to excuse | /ɪks'kju:z/ |
| breath | /breθ/ | to breathe | /bri:ð/ |
| half | /ha:f/ | to halve | /ha:v/ |
| house | /haʊs/ | to house | /haʊz/ |
| safe | /seɪf/ | to save | /seɪv/ |
| bath | /ba:θ/ | to bathe | /beɪð/ |

**10** 1 **B** I <u>did</u> do it.
2 **B** <u>I</u> did it. Sorry.
3 **B** I knew <u>Johann</u> was coming.
4 **B** I knew that <u>ages</u> ago.
5 **B** <u>I</u> didn't tell her.
6 **B** I <u>didn't</u> tell her.
7 **B** I <u>told</u> you.
8 **B** I like <u>Annie</u>.
9 **B** I <u>do</u> like Annie. I think she's <u>great</u>.
10 **B** <u>I</u> like her.

# OXFORD
UNIVERSITY PRESS

Great Clarendon Street, Oxford OX2 6DP

Oxford University Press is a department of the University of Oxford.
It furthers the University's objective of excellence in research, scholarship,
and education by publishing worldwide in

Oxford New York

Auckland Cape Town Dar es Salaam Hong Kong Karachi
Kuala Lumpur Madrid Melbourne Mexico City Nairobi
New Delhi Shanghai Taipei Toronto

With offices in

Argentina Austria Brazil Chile Czech Republic France Greece
Guatemala Hungary Italy Japan Poland Portugal Singapore
South Korea Switzerland Thailand Turkey Ukraine Vietnam

OXFORD and OXFORD ENGLISH are registered trade marks of
Oxford University Press in the UK and in certain other countries

ISBN: 978 0 19 439301 0

Printed in China

This book is printed on paper from certified and well-managed sources.

ACKNOWLEDGEMENTS

*The authors and publisher are grateful to those who have given permission to reproduce
the following extracts and adaptations of copyright material:* p6 'A Vision of the High
Life' by Clare Chapman, The Sunday Times, 18 January 2004. Reproduced by
kind permission of Clare Chapman; p54 'The Thrill Seeker' reproduced from
Radio Times Magazine, 2–9 July 2004; p72 Philippa Forrester's 'My First
Crash' as told to Mark Anstead, published 4 July 2004 in The Sunday Times.
Reproduced by kind permission.

*Illustrations by:* Gill Button p9; Paul Gilligan/Getty Images p48; Ned Jolliffe p69;
Roger Penwill p58; Harry Venning pp38, 71.

*Commissiond Photography by:* Pierre d'Alancaisez p34; Mark Mason p47

*The publisher would like to thank the following for their permission to reproduce
photographs and other copyright material:* Alamy Images pp23 (school kids/Janine
Wiedel Photolibrary), 32 (man at desk/Pictor International), 50
(Concorde/Richard Cooke), 50 (Angel Falls/Jacques Jangoux), 51
(Algarve/Travel-Shots), 63 (man on phone/FogStock), 71 (woman,
man/imageshop), 79 (windsurfer/Steve Austin); Anthony Blake Photo Library
p53 (gateau/Gerrit Buntrock); Axiom Photographic Agency pp16
(backpackers/Paul Quayle), 50 (Petronas Towers/Mary Winch); Capital
Pictures p46 ('Mean Girls'filmstill); Cartoon Stock Ltd pp8 (shopping/Richard
Jolley), 11 (car/Adey Bryant), 15 (waiter/Patrick Hardin), 18 (babysitter/Marc
Tyler Nobleman), 24 (answerphone/Hatley Schwadron), 29 (goldfish/Robert
Thompson), 36 (couple/Marc Tyler Nobleman), 39 (advertising/John Morris),
65 (customs/Roy Nixon), 74 (cat/Matt Percival); Corbis pp5 (beach/Michael S.
Yamashita), 12 (woman climber/John Van Hasselt), 21 (Shrek/Eriko
Sugita/Reuters), 25 (exam results/Ian Hodgson/Reuters), 26 (Frank
Abagnale/Reuters), 42 (fashion show/Petre Buzoianu), 50 (Pygmy
family/Martin Harvey), 77 (girl at computer/LWA-JDC); Coreyography LLC
images p13; Exley Publications, Fiddy's Guide to Husbands, pp29 (How to
Lose Weight), 31, 57, 78, 80; Geoff Mackley p54; Getty Editorial p56 (The
Hives/Matt Carmichael); Getty Images pp28 (friends/Jean Louis Batt/Taxi), 33
(couple/Photodisc), 79 (woman splashing/Zigy Kaluzny/The Image Bank);
Impact Photos Ltd p40 (Ethiopia street scene/Caroline Penn, Odonga
Bosko/Victoria Ivleva); Kobal Collection pp26 (Catch Me if You Can film still
and poster/Dreamworks); OUP pp32 (New York/Photodisc), 45
(woman/Photodisc), 55 (rainbow/Photodisc), 64 (Taj Mahal/Photodisc); Mrs
PJM Bevan p60; Punchstock pp5 (man on mobile/Medioimages), 10
(men/Image Source), 15 (couple/Image Source/Goodshoot), 17
(camping/Corbis), 19 (man with paddle/Photodisc), 22 (pile of
books/Photodisc), 32 (daydreaming student/Digital Vision), 35
(kitchen/Photodisc), 37 (traffic jam/imageshop), 43
(businessman/Medioimages), 49 (two women/Image Source), 62 (couple/IT
Stock Free), 67 (teens with dog/image100), 68 (having coffee/Brand X
Pictures), 71 (mature man/Rubberball), 72 (driving/image100), 76 (two men/IT
Stock free), 82 (couple with laptop/IT Stock); Rex Features pp30 (Tom
Hanks/Charles Sykes), 53 (Glastonbury/Steve Meddle), 72 (Phillipa
Forrester/Nils Jorgensen); Studio Aisslinger p6.

# Phonetic symbols

## Consonants

| | | | | |
|---|---|---|---|---|
| 1 | /p/ | as in | **pen** | /pen/ |
| 2 | /b/ | as in | **big** | /bɪg/ |
| 3 | /t/ | as in | **tea** | /tiː/ |
| 4 | /d/ | as in | **do** | /duː/ |
| 5 | /k/ | as in | **cat** | /kæt/ |
| 6 | /g/ | as in | **go** | /gəʊ/ |
| 7 | /f/ | as in | **four** | /fɔː/ |
| 8 | /v/ | as in | **very** | /ˈveri/ |
| 9 | /s/ | as in | **son** | /sʌn/ |
| 10 | /z/ | as in | **zoo** | /zuː/ |
| 11 | /l/ | as in | **live** | /lɪv/ |
| 12 | /m/ | as in | **my** | /maɪ/ |
| 13 | /n/ | as in | **near** | /nɪə/ |
| 14 | /h/ | as in | **happy** | /ˈhæpi/ |
| 15 | /r/ | as in | **red** | /red/ |
| 16 | /j/ | as in | **yes** | /jes/ |
| 17 | /w/ | as in | **want** | /wɒnt/ |
| 18 | /θ/ | as in | **thanks** | /θæŋks/ |
| 19 | /ð/ | as in | **the** | /ðə/ |
| 20 | /ʃ/ | as in | **she** | /ʃiː/ |
| 21 | /ʒ/ | as in | **television** | /ˈtelɪvɪʒn/ |
| 22 | /tʃ/ | as in | **child** | /tʃaɪld/ |
| 23 | /dʒ/ | as in | **German** | /ˈdʒɜːmən/ |
| 24 | /ŋ/ | as in | **English** | /ˈɪŋglɪʃ/ |

## Vowels

| | | | | |
|---|---|---|---|---|
| 25 | /iː/ | as in | **see** | /siː/ |
| 26 | /ɪ/ | as in | **his** | /hɪz/ |
| 27 | /i/ | as in | **twenty** | /ˈtwenti/ |
| 28 | /e/ | as in | **ten** | /ten/ |
| 29 | /æ/ | as in | **stamp** | /stæmp/ |
| 30 | /ɑː/ | as in | **father** | /ˈfɑːðə/ |
| 31 | /ɒ/ | as in | **hot** | /hɒt/ |
| 32 | /ɔː/ | as in | **morning** | /ˈmɔːnɪŋ/ |
| 33 | /ʊ/ | as in | **football** | /ˈfʊtbɔːl/ |
| 34 | /uː/ | as in | **you** | /juː/ |
| 35 | /ʌ/ | as in | **sun** | /sʌn/ |
| 36 | /ɜː/ | as in | **learn** | /lɜːn/ |
| 37 | /ə/ | as in | **letter** | /ˈletə/ |

## Diphthongs (two vowels together)

| | | | | |
|---|---|---|---|---|
| 38 | /eɪ/ | as in | **name** | /neɪm/ |
| 39 | /əʊ/ | as in | **no** | /nəʊ/ |
| 40 | /aɪ/ | as in | **my** | /maɪ/ |
| 41 | /aʊ/ | as in | **how** | /haʊ/ |
| 42 | /ɔɪ/ | as in | **boy** | /bɔɪ/ |
| 43 | /ɪə/ | as in | **hear** | /hɪə/ |
| 44 | /eə/ | as in | **where** | /weə/ |
| 45 | /ʊə/ | as in | **tour** | /tʊə/ |